Joseph Jones

Researches upon Spurious Vaccination

or the abnormal phenomena accompanying and following vaccination in the confederat army, during the american civil war 1861 - 1865

Joseph Jones

Researches upon Spurious Vaccination
or the abnormal phenomena accompanying and following vaccination in the confederat army, during the american civil war 1861 - 1865

ISBN/EAN: 9783742818645

Manufactured in Europe, USA, Canada, Australia, Japa

Cover: Foto ©ninafisch / pixelio.de

Manufactured and distributed by brebook publishing software (www.brebook.com)

Joseph Jones

Researches upon Spurious Vaccination

RESEARCHES

UPON

"SPURIOUS VACCINATION,"

OR THE

ABNORMAL PHENOMENA ACCOMPANYING AND FOLLOWING VACCINATION

IN THE

Confederate Army,

DURING THE RECENT

AMERICAN CIVIL WAR, 1861--1865.

BY

JOSEPH JONES, M.D.,

Professor of Physiology and Pathology in the Medical Department of the University of Nashville, Tenn.

From the Nashville Journal of Medicine and Surgery.

Nashville, Tenn.:
UNIVERSITY MEDICAL PRESS—W. H. F. LIGON, PRINTER.
1867.

RESEARCHES

Upon *"Spurious Vaccination,"* or the Abnormal Phenomena accompanying and following Vaccination in the Confederate Army, during the recent American Civil War, 1861–1865. By JOSEPH JONES, M.D., Professor of Physiology and Pathology, in the Medical Department of the University of Nashville, Tenn.

SECTION I.

PRELIMINARY OBSERVATIONS—ACCIDENTS ATTENDING VACCINATION AMONGST THE CITIZENS AND SOLDIERS OF THE CONFEDERATE STATES—NECESSITY FOR THE INVESTIGATION—METHOD, EXTENT AND OBJECT OF THE INQUIRY.

During the recent civil war, untoward results followed vaccination, and a number of deaths both amongst the troops and citizens were directly referable to the effects of vaccination. So great was the evil in the army, that it was made a special subject of investigation, and a number of interesting reports were prepared by several of the medical officers, upon what was most generally called in the army, "spurious vaccination." Our friend, Surgeon Jackson Chambliss, in charge of Div. No. 1 Camp Winder Hospital, Richmond, had examined and recorded a large number of cases of "spurious vaccination," illustrated with drawings of the various local diseases and skin affections. As far as our information extends, this valuable mass of matter, relating to one of the most important subjects in its bearings upon the welfare of the human race, was destroyed during the evacuation of Richmond. If any of these reports are still in existence, we shall be happy to be the medium of communicating them to the profession.

So common had accidents become after vaccination, and so strong was the prejudice growing, both in the army and amongst citizens against its employment, that we instituted a series of experiments upon the inoculation of cows with small-pox matter, in order to produce, if possible, cow-pox, from whence a supply of fresh and reliable vaccine matter might be obtained. It was our design to carry out an extensive series of investigations upon the various secondary affections following vaccination, and to determine, if possible, what contagious principles could be associated with the lymph of the vaccine vesicle. These labors were brought to a sudden and unexpected close, by the disastrous termination of the civil war. As far, however, as our labors amongst the Confederate troops extended, we were led to attribute the injurious effects of vaccination to the following causes:

1st.—*Depressed forces, consequent upon fatigue and exposure and poor diet: impoverished, vitiated and scorbutic condition of the blood of the patients vaccinated, or yielding vaccine matter.*

2d.—*The employment of matter from pustules or ulcers which had deviated from the regular and usual course of development of the vaccine vesicle; such deviation or imperfection in the vaccine disease or pustule being due mainly to previous vaccination, and the existence of some eruptive disease at the time of vaccination. Or in other words, the employment of matter from patients who had been previously vaccinated, and who were affected with some skin disease at the the time of the insertion of the vaccine virus.*

3d.—*Dried Vaccine, Lymph or Scabs, in which decomposition has been excited by carrying the matter about the person for a length of time, and thus subjecting it to a warm moist atmosphere.*

4TH.—*The mingling of the Vaccine Virus with that of the Small Pox:*—*matter taken from those who were vaccinated while they were laboring under the action of the poison of Small Pox, was capable of producing a modified Variola, and comparatively mild disease in the inoculated, and was capable of communicating by effluvia Small Pox in its worst character to the unprotected.*

5TH.—*Dried Vaccine, Lymph or Scabs, from patients who had suffered with Erysipelas during the progress of the Vaccine Disease, or whose systems were in a depressed state from improper diet, bad ventilation, and the exhalations from Typhoid Fever, Erysipelas, Hospital Gangrene, Pyœmia, and offensive suppurating wounds.*

6TH.—*Fresh and dried Vaccine Lymph and Scabs, from patients suffering from Syphilis, at the time, and during the progress of vaccination and the vaccine diseases.*

The results of my investigations during the war, were published in the Southern Medical and Surgical Journal, July, 1866, pp. 165-180, under the head of "Spurious Vaccination."

Since the publication of this article, we have still farther investigated the subject, and addressed a large number of communications relating to "Spurious Vaccination" to southern physicians formerly connected with the Confederate Army, and the replies to these inquiries will be found in the following pages; and in truth, aside from the great interest and importance which everything relating to vaccination possesses, one of the chief objects which we had in preparing the present article, was to collect and consolidate and preserve the labors of southern physicians.

The following is the general form of circular employed:

No. 7 NORTH VINE STREET, NASHVILLE, TENN.
—————————— 1866.
——————————M.D.

DEAR SIR:—

I am at present engaged in drawing up a monograph upon "Spurious Vaccination, and "Modified Inoculation."

In this paper, which will be published at an early day, I will endeavor to do full justice to the valuable labors of Confederate Surgeons.

In the circumscribed and distressed condition of the Southern States, cut off from the surrounding world, with the necessity of Vaccinating the entire male population capable of bearing arms, and without any means of obtaining fresh and reliable matter outside of the Confederate States, the experience of the Medical Officers of the Confederate Army possesses a high and peculiar value.

I shall be glad to receive from you a communication, setting forth your views at length upon the nature and value of Modified Inoculation, and *upon the* NATURE *and* CAUSES *of the* ACCIDENTS *resulting from* VACCINATION ("SPURIOUS VACCINATION") *in the Confederate Army.*

The subject of the TRANSMISSON *of* SYPHILIS *through the medium of the* VACCINE VIRUS, should be carefully discussed, and all conclusions should be supported by carefully recorded *facts* and *cases*. *One* well reported *case*, proving the transmission of *Constitutional Syphilis*, or any other disease, as *Erysipelas*, by vaccination, is worth large volumes of mere opinions and assertions.

We should exercise the utmost caution in discussing the value of vaccination, and the causes of the accidents, which have tended of late, to bring it into disrepute with the public; for all conscientious physicians and lovers of mankind will agree that this question is interesting, not only to the physiologist and medical practitioner, but that it concerns every community on the earth, and comes home to every individual of the human race.

It has been well said, by a writer who was not a medical man, "It is difficult to conceive that there should be one being who would not be affected by its decision, either in his own person, or by those of his nearest connexions. To the bulk of mankind wars and revolutions are things of infinitely less importance; and even to those who busy themselves in the tumult of public affairs, it may be doubted whether any thing can occur that will command so powerful and permanant an interest, since there are few to whom fame or freedom can be so intimately and constantly precious as personal safety and domestic affection."

It is important that we should carefully distinguish the accidents which result from carelessness in the selection of the matter, and from ignorance of the true character and progress of the vaccine disease,

You will oblige me by answering at an early day, and also by forwarding the address of any physicians who have made this subject a special study, and who have recorded trustworthy observations.

Very respectfully yours,

JOSEPH JONES.

This circular letter has not been as widely distributed as was desired; as it has been difficult to ascertain the address of many of the medical officers of the Southern Army, on account of the sudden manner, in which the struggle terminated, and the utter and sudden loss of all organization and records; and on account of the imperfect mail facilities of the Southern States.

Therefore, all who may receive this paper, are respectfully requested to consider themselves as addressed in person.

The replies which have been received in response to my letters, will be found under the different divisions of the inquiry; and we have preferred presenting each paper entire, when using it for the illustration of some particular branch of the subject, although it might contain some matter irrelevant to the subject under immediate consideration. In this manner we hoped to do entire justice to those contributing facts and observations; and whilst we have freely expressed the results of our investigation, and given our judgment without reserve, we have endeavored on the other hand to avoid all personal criticism. The replies to these printed enquiries will be published from time to time as they may be received.

Before proceeding to the discussion of the subjects under consideration, it is but just that I should disclaim all design of decrying vaccination when properly performed. Nothing is farther from my intention, than even in the remotest manner, to detract from the value of the greatest physical boon ever bestowed by a mortal upon the human race.

From authentic documents and accurate calculations, it has been ascertained that *one* in fourteen, of all that were born died of the small-pox, even after inoculation had been introduced; and of persons of all ages taken ill of the small-pox in the natural way, one in five or six died; and in addition to this frightful mortality, alike observable in all the different regions of the globe, many of those who recovered were permanently disfigured, or deprived of eyesight, or left with shattered constitutions the prey to pulmonary consumption, chronic opthalmia and scrofula.

According to the researches of Black, Lüssmileh and Frank, eight or nine per cent. of the human race were carried off by small-pox: and Duvillard endeavored to show that of 100 persons, only four reached the age of thirty years without having it, that one in seven or eight, who were affected, died; and that of those who were attacked in infancy only two-thirds escaped. Before the introduction of vaccination, small-pox was infinitely more destructive to human life than the plague itself; it has swept away whole tribes of savage and half civilized people, and its miserable victims have been abandoned by their nearest relatives and friends, as persons doomed by divine wrath to irrevocable death: it was calculated that 210,000 fell victims to it annually in Europe, and Bernouilli believed that not less than fifteen millions of human beings were destroyed by small-pox every twenty-five years, that is six hundred thousand annually: and this loathsome disease was not only universal in its ravages, but was so subtle in its influence and insidious in its attack, that all efforts to stay its violence or to prevent its approach, were utterly futile. Even inoculation whilst it was far less severe and fatal than the natural small-pox and thus benefitted the indiviual, tended nevertheless to increase the spread of the disease, and its extensive adoption was attended with a most marked increase of mortality of the disease in the human race.

Sir Matthew Hale in a letter of advice and admonition to one of his grandsons, has given an excellent picture of this disease, which well illustrates its odious characters, and exhibits the impression which it makes upon the world at large, in a stronger light than if the description had been drawn up by a strictly professional hand.

"First, therefore, touching your late sickness (small-pox) I would have you remember these particulars: 1st. The disease itself in its own nature is now become ordinary very mortal, especially to those of your age. Look upon even the last year's general bill of mortality, you will find near two thousand dead of that disease the last year; and, had God not been merciful to you, you might have been one of that number with as great likelihood as any of them who died of that disease. 2d. It was a contagious disease that secluded the access of your nearest relations. 3d. Your sickness surprised you upon a sudden, when you seemed to be in your full strength. 4th. Your sickness rendered you noisome to yourself and all that were about you; and a spectacle full of deformity, by the excess of your disease, beyond most that are sick thereof. 5th. It was a fierce and violent sickness: it did not only take away the common supplies of nature, as digestion, sleep, strength, but it took away your memory, your understanding and the very sense of your condition, or of what might be conducible to your good. All that you could do was only to 'make your condition more desperate, in case they that were about you had not prevented it and taken more care for you than you did or could for yourself. 6th. Your sickness was desperate, in so much that your symptoms and the violence of your distemper were without example; and you were in the very next degree to absolute rottenness, putrefaction and death itself."

By the unaided efforts of a man, emulous not of distinction but desirous of advancing truth, and promoting the happiness and well being of his fellow creatures, and distinguished as much for his humility, long suffering and perservence, as for his unsurpassed powers of practical observation, the world has been furnished with the means of completely eradicating this terrible scourge, by substituting the same disease in a mild, modified form non-communicable by effluvia and capable of affording complete immunity from the natural small-pox.

So far, therefore, from charging the accidents which we are about to describe, to the process of vaccination, as established and advocated by Edward Jenner, we are persuaded that a very large part, if not the whole of these distressing accidents and failures, are to be ascribed directly or indirectly to the ignorance, and inattention, of those who practice vaccination. We have no more sympathy with the modern opponents of vaccination, than we have with those English physicians who attempted to decry the labors and to steal the honest dues of their immortal countryman, and who condescended to such low expedients as to caricature the process of vaccination, by representing the human visage under its effects, in the act of transformation into that of the lower animals, the cow and the horse. And we would heartily endorse any public enactment which would guard in a proper manner the process of vaccination ; and at the present time some of the older European edicts upon the subject of vaccination, as those of the Emperor of Russia in 1811, and of the King of Wirtemburgh in 1818, might be reënacted by the General and State Governments, with great benefit to the people.

If the profession had uniformly adhered to the advice and the rules established by the illustrious founder of vaccination, we would have been spared the vast majority of the unfortunate accidents which tend to bring this, the only safeguard against the small-pox, into disrepute.

Dr. Jenner gave the most minute attention to every deviation from the correct progress of the vaccine vesicle, to the state of the virus to be inserted, to the condition of the skin of the person about to be vaccinated, and to the character of the vesicle itself; and so early as the year 1799, had ascertained by the clearest evidence, some of the causes of accident and failure, which have been confirmed by later observations.

He showed that in some cases the system was not rendered totally unsusceptible to the variolous contagion, either by the cow-pox vaccination, or the small-pox; but that vaccination, when properly performed with genuine matter, afforded as complete protection as the small-pox itself. He proved that by inoculating a person who had gone through the cow-pox, with variolous matter, it was possible to excite a local vesication, the virus from which was capable of producing a mild but efficacious small-pox. He farther maintained that modifications and varieties might arise in the vaccine pustule, and that these varieties were such as to produce "every gradation in the state of the pustule, from that slight deviation from perfection, which is quite immaterial, up to that point which affords no security at all." He held that fluid taken from a spurious vaccine pustule can propagate and perpetuate its like, and even if it be taken from a genuine pustule in its far-advanced stages, it is capable of producing varieties which will be permanent if we continue to employ it.

Jenner laid great stress upon the herpetic state of the skin, in inducing deviation in the normal progress of the vaccine disease; but every deviation, from whatever cause it may have arisen, was considered by him of the greatest moment; and in all his published works, as well as in his private communications and letters, he never failed to urge the importance of the most scrupulous attention to the mode of propagation and to the whole progress of the vaccine disease.

Thus in his paper on the "Varieties and Modifications of the Vaccine Pustule," he thus urges upon the profession the necessity of the most careful attention to this important subject:

"I shall conclude this paper by observing that although vaccine inoculation does not inflict a severe disease, but, on the contrary, produces a mild affection, scarcely meriting the term *disease*, yet, nevertheless, the inoculator should be extremely careful to obtain a just and clear conception of this important branch of medical science. He should not only be acquainted with the laws and agencies of the vaccine virus on the constitution, but with those of the variolous also, as they often interfere with each other.

"A general knowledge of the subject is not sufficient to enable us to warrant a person to practice vaccine inoculation: he should possess a peculiar knowledge; and that which I would wish strongly to inculcate, as the great foundation of the whole, is an intimate acquaintance with the character of the true and genuine pustule. The spurious pustule would then be readily detected, whatever form it might assume; and errors known no more."

Dr. Jenner, in a letter written to Sir Gilbert, near the close of his life, reïterates these precautions, and observes:

"With regard to the mitigated disease which sometimes follows vaccination, I can positively say, and shall be borne out in my assertion by those who are in future days to follow me, that it is the offspring entirely of incaution in those who conduct the vaccine process. On what does the inexplicable change which guards the constitution from the fang of the small-pox depend? On nothing but a correct state of the pustule on the arm excited by the insertion of the virus; and why are these pustules sometimes incorrect, losing their characteristic shape, and performing their offices partially?"—*(Life of Edward Jenner, M.D., L.L.D., etc., by John Baron, M.D., Vol. ii., p. 241.)*

Jenner even went so far as to maintain that the process of vaccination might be rendered ineffective by mechanically disturbing the vesicle, during the collection and transmission of the virus, and he insisted upon the necessity of allowing one vesicle at least to run its course undisturbed.

So far, therefore, from desiring to injure the cause of vaccination by the record of distressing failures and accidents, it will be our endeavor, rather in the spirit of Jenner. to guard the process, by so exposing the cause of these accidents as to lead to their avoidance in future.

"Ere I proceed, let me be permitted to observe, that truth in this, and every other physiological inquiry that has occupied my attention, has ever been the first object of my pursuit; and should it appear in the present instance that I have been led into error, fond as I may appear of the offspring of my labors, I had rather see it perish at once than exist and do a public injury."

SECTION II.

MODIFICATION, ALTERATION AND DEGENERATION OF THE VACCINE VESICLE, DEPENDENT UPON DEPRESSED AND DERANGED

FORCES, RESULTING FROM FATIGUE, EXPOSURE AND POOR DIET; AND UPON AN IMPOVERISHED, VITIATED AND SCORBUTIC CONDITION OF THE BLOOD OF THE PATIENTS VACCINATED AND YIELDING VACCINE MATTER. IN SCORBUTIC PATIENTS ALL INJURIES OF THE SKIN TEND TO FORM ULCERS OF AN UNHEALTHY CHARACTER. EFFECTS OF SCURVY UPON THE CHARACTER AND PROGRESS OF THE VACCINE VESICLE. INVESTIGATIONS UPON THE EFFECTS OF VACCINATION AMONGST THE FEDERAL PRISONERS CONFINED IN CAMP SUMPTER, ANDERSONVILLE, GA. LETTER AND REPORT ON SPURIOUS VACCINATION, BY DR. S. E. HABERSHAM.

Large numbers of the Confederate soldiers manifested slight scorbutic symptoms, which were not sufficient to attract attention, or to induce treatment, and as far as we could learn, no attention was paid to this condition either in vaccination or in the selection of the vaccine lymph.

In scorbutic patients, all injuries tended to form ulcers of an unhealthy character, and the vaccine vesicles even when they appeared at the proper time, and manifested many of the usual symptoms of the vaccine disease, were nevertheless larger and more slow in healing, and the scabs presented an enlarged, scaly, dark, unhealthy appearance. In many cases, a large ulcer covered with a thick laminated crust, from one-quarter to one inch in diameter, followed the introduction of the vaccine matter into scorbutic patients. Matter from these scabs and sores was frequently used in vaccination, and this decomposing pus and blood acted as an animal poison in some cases, and especially in constitutions debilitated by exposure, fatigue, and salt diet.

During the prosecution of the investigations which we instituted upon the diseases of the Federal prisoners confined at Andersonville, the opportunity was embraced of investigating the remarkable effects which followed the attempts of the Confederate medical officers to arrest the spread of small-pox by vaccination. In a number of cases, large gangrenous ulcers appeared at the points where the vaccine lymph had been inserted, causing extensive destruction of tissues, exposing arteries, nerves, and bones, and necessitating amputation in more than one instance. These accidents led to the belief amongst some of the prisoners that the Surgeons had intentionally introduced poisonous matter into their arms during vaccination.

After careful inquiry we were led to the conclusion that these accidents were, in the case of these Federal prisoners, referable wholly to the scorbutic condition of their blood, and to the crowded condition of the stockade and hospital. The smallest accidental injuries and abrasions of the surface, as from splinters, or bites of insects, were in a number of instances followed by such extensive gangrene as to necessitate amputation. The gangrene following vaccination appeared to be due essentially to the same cause; and in the condition of the blood of these patients, would most probably have attacked any puncture made by a lancet, without any vaccine matter or any other extraneous material. It appeared also that the dried scab, resulting from the vaccination of these scorbutic patients, was also capable of producing effects wholly different from the vaccine lymph of healthy individuals; and in some cases these effects were of a most potent and injurious character.

The cause of JUSTICE and TRUTH, demands at my hands, something more, than this simple record, with reference to the *accidents* following *vaccination*, amongst the Federal prisoners confined in Camp Sumpter.

In the specification of the first charge against Henry Wirz, formerly Commandant of the interior of the Confederate States Military Prison, during his *Trial* before a *Special Military Commission*, convened in accordance with Special Orders No. 453, War Department, Adjutant General's Office, Washington, August 23, 1865, the following is written:

"And the said Wirz, still pursuing his wicked purpose, and still aiding in carrying out said conspiracy, did use and cause to be used, for the pretended purpose of vaccination, impure and poisonous matter, which said impure and poisonous matter was then and there, by the direction and order of said Wirz, maliciously, cruelly, and wickedly deposited in the arms of many of said prisoners, by reason of which large numbers of them, to-wit, one hundred, lost the use of their arms, and many of them, to-wit, about the number of two hundred, were so injured that they soon thereafter died: All of which he, the said Henry Wirz, well knew and maliciously intended, and in aid of the then existing rebellion against the United States, with the view to assist in weakening and impairing the armies of the United States, and in furtherance of the said conspiracy, and with full knowledge, consent and connivance of his co-conspirators aforesaid, he the said Wirz, then and there did."

Amongst the co-conspirators specified in the charges, were the Surgeon of the Post, Dr. White, and the Surgeon in charge of the Military Prison Hospital, R. R. Stevenson. As the vaccinations were made by their orders, and by the medical officers of the Confederate Army acting under their command, the charge of deliberately poisoning the Federal Prisoners with vaccine matter, is a sweeping one, and whether intended so or not, affects every medical officer stationed at that post; and it appears to have been designed to go farther and to affect the reputation of every one who held a commission in the Medical Department of the Confederate Army.

The acts of those who once composed the Medical Department of the Confederate Army, from the efficient and laborious Surgeon General to the Regimental officers, need no defence at my hands: time, with its unerring lines of historic truth, will embalm their heroic labors in the cause of suffering humanity, and will acknowledge their untiring efforts to ameliorate the most gigantic mass of suffering, that ever fell to the lot of a beleaguered and distressed people.

I desire at the present time, simply to place on record, the results of labors which concern this country, no more than any other; and these results when properly received without prejudice or malicious hatred, will be seen to relate to the hygiene and to the diseases of Prisoners, however confined, and wherever incarcerated, in civil or military prisons throughout the world.

In accordance with the direction of Dr. Samuel Preston Moore, formerly Surgeon General C. S. A., I instituted during the months of August and September, 1864, a series of investigations upon the diseases of Federal Prisoners confined in Camp Sumpter, Andersonville, Georgia.

The field was of great extent and of extraordinary importance. There were more than five thousand seriously sick in the hospital and stockade, and the deaths ranged from ninety, to one hundred and thirty, each day. From the establishment of the Prison, on the 24th of February, 1864, to the 1st of October, over ten thousand Federal prisoners died : that is, near one-third of the entire number perished in less than seven months. I instituted careful investigations into the condition of the sick and well, and performed numerous post-mortem examinations, and executed drawings of the diseased structures. The medical topography of Andersonville and of the surrounding country was examined, and the waters of the streams, springs and wells, around and within the stockade and hospital carefully analyzed.

The report which I drew up for the use of the Medical Department of the Confederate Army, contained a truthful representation of the sufferings of these prisoners, and at the same time gave an equally truthful view of the difficulties, under which the medical officers labored, and of the distressed, and beleaguered and desolated condition of the Southern States. Shortly after the close of the civil war, this report, which had never been delivered, on account of the destruction of all railroad communication with Richmond, Virginia, was suddenly seized by the agents of the United States government, conducting the trial to which we have alluded.

It was with extreme pain that I contemplated the diversion of my labors, in the cause of Medical science, from their true and legitimate object, and I addressed an earnest appeal, which accompanied the report, to the Judge Advocate, Col. N. P. Chipman, in which I used the following language :

In justice to myself, as well as to those most nearly connected with this investigation, I would respectfully call the attention of Col. Chipman, Judge Advocate U. S. A., to the fact that the matter which is surrendered in obedience to the demands of a power from which there is no appeal, was prepared solely for the consideration of the Surgeon General, C. S. A., and was designed to promote the cause of humanity, and to advance the interests of the Medical profession. This being granted, I feel assured that the Judge Advocate will appreciate the deep pain which the anticipation gives me that these labors may be diverted from their original mission, and applied to the prosecution of criminal cases. The same principle which led me to endeavor to deal humanely and justly by these suffering prisoners, and to make a truthful representation of their condition to the Medical Department of the Confederate Army, now actuates me in recording my belief that as far as my knowledge extends, there was no deliberate or willful design on the part of the Chief

Executive, Jefferson Davis, and the highest authorities of the Confederate Government to injure the health and destroy the lives of these Federal Prisoners.

On the 21st of May, 1861, it was enacted by the "Congress of the Confederate States of America," "That all prisoners of war taken, whether on land or at sea, during the pending hostilities with the United States, should be transferred by the captors, from time to time, as often as convenient, to the Department of War; and it shall be the duty of the Secretary of War, with the approval of the President, to issue such instructions to the Quartermaster General and his subordinates, as shall provide for the safe custody and sustenance of prisoners of war; and the rations furnished prisoners of war shall be the same in quantity and quality as those furnished enlisted men in the army of the Confederacy." By act of February 17, 1864 the Quartermaster General was relieved of this duty, and the Commissary General of Subsistence was ordered to provide for the sustenance of prisoners of war.

According to General Orders No. 159, Adjutant and Inspector General's Office, "hospitals for prisoners of war are placed on the same footing as other Confederate States hospitals, in all respects, and will be managed accordingly."

The Federal prisoners were removed to South-western Georgia in the early part of 1864, not only to secure a place of confinement more remote than Richmond and other large towns, from the operations of the United States forces, *but also to secure a more abundant and easy supply of food.*

As far as my experience extends, no person who had been reared upon wheat bread, and who was held in captivity for any length of time, could retain his health and escape either scurvy or diarrhœa, if confined to the Confederate ration (issued to the soldier in the field and hospital) of unbolted corn meal and bacon. The large armies of the Confederacy suffered more than once from scurvy, and as the war progressed, secondary hemorrhage and hospital gangrene became fearfully prevalent, from the deteriorated condition of the systems of the troops, dependent upon the prolonged use of salt meat. And but for the extra supplies received from home and from the various benevolent State institutions, scurvy and diarrhœa and dysentery would have been still farther prevalent."

It was believed by the citizens of the Southern States, that the Confederate authorities desired to effect a continuous, and speedy exchange of prisoners of war in their hands, on the ground that the retention of these soldiers in captivity was a great calamity, not only entailing heavy expenditure of the scanty means of subsistence, already insufficient to support their suffering, half-starved, half-clad and unpaid armies, struggling in the field with overwhelming numbers, and embarrassing their imperfect and dilapidated lines of communication; but also as depriving them of the services of a veteran army fully equal to one-third the numbers actively engaged in the field; and the history of subsequent events have shown that the retention in captivity of the Confederate prisoners was one of the efficient causes of the final and complete overthrow of the Confederate Government. * * *

It is my honest belief that if the exhausted condition of the Confederate Government, with its bankrupt currency, with its retreating and constantly diminishing armies, with the apparent impossibility of filling up the vacancies by death and desertion and sickness, and of gathering a guard of reserves of sufficient strength to allow of the proper enlargement of the Military Prison, and with a country torn and bleeding along all its borders with its starving women and children and old men fleeing from the desolating march of contending armies, crowding the dilapidated and over-burdened railroad lines, and adding to the distress and consuming the poor charities of those in the interior, who were harrassed by the loss of sons and brothers and husbands, and by the fearful visions of starvation and undefined misery, could be fully realized, much of the suffering of the Federal prisoners would be attributed to csuses connected with the distressed condition of the Southern States.

It was clearly demonstrated in my report that diarrhœa, dysentery, scurvy and hospital gangrene were the diseases which caused the extraordinary mortality of Andersonville. And it was still farther shown that this mortality was referable, in no appreciable degree, to either the character of the soil, or waters, or the conditions of climate.

The effects of salt meat and farinaceous food, without fresh vegetables, were manifest in the great prevalence of scurvy. The scorbutic condition thus induced, modified the course of every disease, poisoned every wound, however slight, and lay at the foundation of those obstinate and exhausting diarrhœas and dysenteries, which swept off thousands of these unfortunate men. By a long and painful investigation of the diseases of these prisoners, supported by numerous post-mortem examinations, I demonstrated conclusively that scurvy induced nine-tenths of the deaths. Not only were the deaths registered as due to unknown causes, to apoplexy, to anasarca, and to debility, directly traceable to scurvy and its effects, and not only was the mortality in small-pox and pneumonia and typhoid fever, and in all acute diseases more than doubled by the scorbutic taint, but even those all but universal and deadly bowel affections, arose from the same causes, and derived their fatal characters from the same conditions which produced the scurvy.

Scurvy and hospital gangrene frequently existed in the same individual. In such cases, vegetable diet, with vegetable acids, would remove the scorbutic condition without curing the hospital gangrene. It has been well established by the observations of Blane, Trotter and others, that the scorbutic condition of the system, especially in crowded camps, ships, hospitals and beleaguered cities, is most favorable to the origin and spread of foul ulcers and hospital gangrene. In many cases occurring amongst the Federal prisoners at Andersonville, it was difficult to decide at first whether the ulcer was a simple result of the scorbutic state, or of the action of the poison of hospital gangrene; for there was great similarity in the appearance of scorbutic ulcers and genuine hospital gangrene. So commonly have these two diseases been combined, that the description of scorbutic ulcers by many authorities, evidently, includes also many of the prominent characteristics of hospital gangrene, as will be seen by a reference to the descriptions of Lind, Trotter, Blane, and others.

More than two hundred and fifty years ago, Paré described a condition of things similar to that of Andersonville: at the siege of Rouen, the air was so noxious that no wounds would heal, and the besieged finding that all their wounds became gangrenous, reported that the besiegers had poisoned the balls; the besiegers also seeing none but putrid sores in the camp, believed that the wounds were poisoned, and both within and without the city such was the state of the air, and so putrid were all the wounds, that the surgeons could scarcely look upon the sores, or endure the smell; and if they neglected them for a single day, they found them filled with worms.

Woodall, in his *Chirurgeons Mate, or Military and Domestic Surgery*, published in 1639, not only carefully describes scorbutic ulcers, but also lays down rules for their treatment; and Gideon Harvey, twenty-four years later, in his "*Venus Unmasked*," mentions superficial, profound, simple, inflamed, callous, dry, sanious, purulent, phagedenick, and gangrenous ulcers, as characteristic of scurvy. This last named author derives the name scurvy from "Scorbeck, and that from Scornobocca, or Fowl mouth, (from Scorno a Fowl or shameful thing, and bocca the mouth), for a stinking breath and fowl rotten gums, may still be termed a foul or shameful mouth; they call it also La marcia di bocca, or putrefaction of the mouth."—p. 24.

The British seamen, in Lord Anson's voyage, and in fact in all long voyages, before the mode of preventing scurvy was practiced, suffered terribly from scorbutic ulcers.

John Huxham in his Essay on Fevers, in the chapter in which he discourses on the "disordered and putrid state of the blood," observes that the

"Salt and half-rotten provisions of sailors in long voyages, cause such a sharpness and corruption of the humors that they are rendered almost unfit for the common uses of life, producing great weakness, languor, wandering pains and aches, stinking breath, corroded, spongy gums, black, blue and sallow spots, sordid, dark, livid fungous ulcers, gangrene, etc., etc. Such scorbutics frequently fall into patecheal fevers, bloody dysenteries, hemorrhages, etc. What is mentioned by the Rev. Mr. Walter in Lord Anson's voyage, is very surprising, viz.: that the blood burst from the wounds of some of the scorbutics after they had been cicatrified for twenty or thirty years. I have known many a ship's company set out on a cruise in high health, and yet in two or three months, return vastly sickly, and eaten out with the scurvy, a third part of them half-rotten and utterly unfit for service. About four or five weeks after they have been out, they begin to drop down, one after another and at length by dozens, till at least scarce half the *compliment* can stand to their duty, particularly I remember some years since, from a squadron under Admiral Martin, we had near 1200 men put on the shore sick at one time, though they went out very healthy and returned in about twelve or thirteen weeks."—p. 47.

Dr. John Hunter, Surgeon in the English Army, in his "Observations on the Diseases of the Army in Jamaica," states that

"Sores and ulcers in the lower extremities were frequent at all seasons of the year and in all the different quarters where the soldiers were stationed. They together with fevers and fluxes, amounted to nineteen-twentieths of the sick received into the hospitals, all other complaints not being more than one-twentieth, if particular times be excepted, when the dry-belly-ache or small-pox were prevalent. The proportion of sores in the hospitals, though always considerable, admitted of great variation. At Spanish Town and Kingston they were often one-third; at Fort Augusta, one-half, and at Stony Hill, two-thirds of the whole number in hospital. They arise from the most trifling causes; a scratch, or hurt, or bruise in the lower extremities, are sufficient to produce a sore, which is always difficult to heal, and sometimes impossible. Old sores often break out anew, and prove equally obstinate."

Dr. Lind, in his valuable work on the scurvy, has recorded the fact that the slightest bruises and wounds of scorbutic persons may degenerate into offensive bloody and fungous ulcers, which are prone to spread with great rapidity, which are cured with the greatest difficulty. The distinguishing characteristics of scorbutic ulcers, as given by Dr. Lind, are as follows:

"They do not afford a good digestion, but a thin fœtid matter, mixed with blood, which at length has the appearance of coagulated blood, and is with great difficulty wiped off or separated from the parts below. The flesh underneath these sloughs feels to the probe soft and spongy. No irritating applications are here of any service: for though such sloughs be with great pains taken away, they are found again at next dressing, when the same bloody appearance always presents itself. Their edges are generally of a livid color and puffed up with excrescences of luxuriant flesh arising under the skin. When too tight a compression is made, in order to keep these excrescences from arising, they are apt to have a gangrenous disposition; and the member never fails to become swelled, painful and for the most part spotted. As the disease increases, they come at length to shoot out a soft bloody fungus, which the sailors express by the name of bullock's liver: and indeed it has a near resemblance, in consistence and color, to that substance when boiled. It often rises in a night's time to a monstrous size, and although destroyed by caustics, or the knife, (in which last case a plentiful bleeding generally ensues), is found at next dressing as large as ever. They continue, however, in this condition a considerable time without tainting the bone. The slightest bruises and wounds of scorbutic persons degenerate sometimes into such ulcers. Their appearances on whatever part of the body, is singular and uniform; and they are easily distinguished from all others, by being so remarkably offensive, bloody and fungous, that we cannot here but take notice of the impropriety of refering many inveterate and obstinate ulcers on the legs, with very different appearances, to scurvy; which are generally best cured by giving mercurial medicines: whereas that medicine in a truly scorbutic ulcer is the most dangerous and pernicious that can be administered."

In like manner Doctor David Macbride in his "Methodical Introduction to the Theory and Practice of Physic," London, 1772, p. 618, affirms that:

"The slightest wounds and bruises in scorbutic people degenerate into foul and untoward ulcers. And the appearance of these ulcers is so singular and uniform that they are easily distinguished from all others. Scorbutic ulcers afford no good digestion, but a thin and fœtid ichor mixed with blood, which at length has the appearance of coagulated gore lying caked on the surface of the sore, and is with great difficulty wiped off or separated from the parts below. The flesh underneath these sloughs feels to the probe soft and spongy, and is very putrid. No detergents nor escharotics are here of any service; for though such sloughs be with great pains taken away, they are found again at the next dressing, where the same sanguinous putrid appearance always presents itself. Their edges are generally of a livid color, and puffed up with excrescences of putrid flesh arising from below the skin. As the violence of the disease increases, the ulcers shoot out a soft bloody fungus, which often rises in a night's time to a monstrous size, and although destroyed by caustics, actual or partial, or cut away with the knife, is found at next dressing as large as ever. It is a good while, however, before these ulcers, bad as they are, come to affect the bone with rottenness."

Sir Gilbert Blane, in his "Observations on the Diseases of Seamen," affirms that there is no complaint more hurtful to the public service, by sea and land, and none more afflicting to the individual than ulcers.

"It is found," says Dr. Blane in the work just referred to, "from direful and multiplied experience, that not only those who are affected with actual symptoms of scurvy, but those who are exposed to the causes of it, and whose constitutions are in such a train as to fall into it, are particularly susceptible of ulcers of the most malignant kind, from the smallest injury which breaks the skin. This might naturally be expected, from what has been said of the great debility of the fibres, and deficiency of the powers of renovation and nutrition in this disease. The characteristic symptoms of such ulcers, are, a thin, fetid discharge, commonly mixed with blood, which sometimes coagulates on the surface. The ulcerated surface is soft and spongy, generally elevated above the level of the surrounding skin, particularly about the edges, where there are excrescences of luxuriant flesh, which in the more advanced state of the ulcer, shoots into a soft bloody fungus, called by the sailors bullock's liver."—*Third Ed., London*, 1799—*p*. 502.

Dr. Blane records a number of important observations showing the tendency to foul gangrenous ulcers amongst seamen. On board the Ganges, of seventy-four guns and six hundred men, during the year 1798, the tendency to the complaint was such that the smallest sore, whether from a hurt or a pimple, fell into the state of an ulcer. Blistered parts were also affected in the same manner. Sores which seemed to be in a healing state, would suddenly become gangrenous. A black speck in the middle was the constant precursor of this. In the most severe cases the ulcers began with violent inflammation, which suddenly terminated in mortification ; destroying in a short time, the fleshy parts, so as to expose the bone, which soon became carious.

The crew of the Triumph, of seventy-four guns and six hundred men, suffered severely from malignant ulcers during the summer and autumn of 1798. Not only wounds and blisters fell nto the ulcerated state, but a scratch or boils and the orifice of the arm after bleeding, were subject to the same accident. Sores which seemed to be in a healing state, would suddenly and without any visible cause, spread again, and become foul and bloody, extremely painful, and would resist every means of cure.

This unfavorable change always began, as in the Ganges, with a black spot in the middle of the ulcer. Ulcers of the same kind prevailed to the most dreadful degree, in the ships serving at the Cape of Good Hope, and in the Naval Hospital there, in the years 1796 and 1797. These foul ulcers produced the most severe and protracted sufferings, terminating frequently in the loss of limbs or life, or both. Nor were they confined to the lower extremities, for the ossa-ilium, the *scapula* and *cranium* would sometimes become *carious*. It became frequently necessary to amputate at the hospital, and it was observed that if the patients who underwent the operation, remained in the wards, with the ulcers, few survived, owing to the gangrenous and ulcerous states of the stumps ; but when they were carried into a separate apartment, the large majority recovered.

It was also observed, both in the ships and at the hospitals, where this species of ulcer prevailed, that the hands of those who dressed them, where the skin was broken, were attacked by the same sort of ulcer.—*Observations on the Diseases of Seamen*, by Gilbert Blane, M.D.—pp. 506–512.

Doctor Thomas Trotter, in his Medicina Nautica, has in like manner, recorded a large number of instances where malignant gangrenous ulcers have arisen spontaneously in various ships, and attacked with violence, not only external injuries ; but in a number of cases, where neither wound, puncture, scab, or contusion could be said to have first taken place, a circumscribed red spot would be first perceived, scarcely to be felt, but in a few hours rising to a pimple, becoming black in the centre and inflamed around the edges, till it increased in size, swelled and assumed every characteristic symptom of malignant ulcer, with constant fever and subsequent ulceration, slough and fetid discharge. This malignant or gangrenous ulcer attacked also the flesh wounds made with the lancet in bleeding, for different inflammatory diseases, as catarrhs and sore-throats. Contused spots, even where the cuticle was not broken, were not exempted from the general tendency to ulceration. But parts that had been scalded or burnt, above all accidents, most quickly assumed the nature of this horrid sore, spread and inflamed more rapidly, and in the end put on the most formidable appearance ; deeper and larger sloughs were the consequence, and symptomatic fever violent in proportion. Even in the early stage, sometimes before the cuticle had burst so as to expose the naked surface, buboes appeared in the groin and axilla, not to be touched without much pain, and always attended with fever. These, however, seldom suppurated ;

but where they did, they constantly exhibited the complexion o the parent sore. (Medicina Nautica, an Essay on the Diseases of Seamen, by Thomas Trotter, M.D., &c., Sec. Ed., 1804, vol. 2d, pp. 169-230; vol. 3d, pp. 467-504).

Dr. Trotter, in the 3d volume states that in the summer of 1799 the malignant ulcer made its appearance on board the Temeraire, with all the characteristic symptoms and violence which marked it in other ships. Every wound, abrasion of the cuticle, blistered part, scald or burn, passed rapidly through the various stages of inflammation, gangrene and sphacelus; in a few days leaving the bones almost bare, from the separation of immense sloughs.

The tendency of the bones to *caries* after inflammation in this disease, was more frequent than in any other species of ulcer, and in many cases rendered the cure very tedious and painful; and many cases sank under the long confinement necessary to the separation of the dead bones.

Dr. George H. B. Macleod, in his "Notes on the Surgery of the War in the Crimea," states that

"The French suffered most dreadfully from hospital gangrene in its worst form. The system they pursued, of removing their wounded and operated cases from the camp to Constantinople at an early date, the pernicious character of the transit, the crowding of their ships and hospitals, all tended to produce the disease, and to render it fatal when produced. Many of their cases commenced in camp, but the majority arose in the hospitals on the Bosphorus, where the disease raged rampant. In the hospitals of the south of France it also prevailed, and, from what M. Lallour, Surgeon to the "Euphrate" transport, tells us in his paper on the subject, it must have committed great ravages in their ships, from one of which, he says, sixty bodies were thrown over during the short passage of thirty-eight hours to the Bosphorus. With them the disease was the true contagious gangrene, and attacked no only open wounds but cicatrixes, and almost every stump in the hospitals."

By the official reports of the medical officers of both the English and French Armies, during the Crimean war, it was conclusively shown that, notwithstanding the extraordinary exertions of these powerful nations, holding undisputed sway of both sea and land, scurvy and a scorbutic condition of the blood, increased to a fearful degree the mortality, not only of gun-shot wounds, but of all diseases, and especially of pneumònia, diarrhœa and dysentery.

We might add many other facts from various authors establishing the spontaneous origin of malignant spreading gangrenous ulcers, in many navies and armies, as the result of scurvy and crowding ; but the facts just recorded are sufficient to show that the foul scorbutic ulcers, and hospital gangrene, and the accidents from vaccination, arising at Andersonville, were by no means new, in the history of medicine, and that the causes which induced these distressing affections have been active in all wars and sieges, and amongst all armies and navies.

In truth these men at Andersonville, were in the condition of a crew at sea, confined upon a foul ship, upon salt meat and unvarying food, and without fresh vegetables. Not only so, but these unfortunate prisoners were like men forcibly confined and crowded upon a ship, tossed about on a stormy ocean, without a rudder, without a compass, without a guiding star, and without any apparent boundary or end to their voyage ; and they reflected in their steadily increasing miseries, the distressed condition and waning fortunes of a devasted and bleeding country, which was compelled, in justice to her own unfortunate sons, to hold these men in this most distressing captivity.

The Federal prisoners received the same rations in kind, quality, and amount, issued to the Confederate soldiers in the field. These rations were, during the last eighteen months of the war, insufficient, and without that variety of fresh meat and vegetables, which would ward off scurvy from soldiers, as well as prisoners.

As far as my experience extended, no body of troops could be confined exclusively to the Confederate rations of 1864 and '65 without manifesting symptoms of the scurvy.

The Confederate ration grew worse and worse as the war progressed, and as portion after portion of the most fertile regions of the Confederate States were overrun and desolated by the Federal Armies. In the straightened condition of the Confederate States, the support of an army of fifty thousand prisoners, forced upon their hands by a relentless policy, was a great and distressing burden, which consumed their scant resources, burdened their rotten lines of railroad, and exhausted the over-taxed energies of the entire country, crowded with refugees from their desolated homes. The Confederate authorities charged with the *exchange of prisoners,* used every effort in their power consistent with their views of national honor and rectitude, to effect an exchange of all prisoners in their hands, and to establish and maintain definite rules by which all prisoners of war might be continuously exchanged as soon as possible after capture.

Whatever the feelings of resentment on the part of the Confederates, may have been, against those who were invading and desolating their native land, which had been purchased by the blood of their ancestors from the Indians and English, the desire for the speedy exchange and return of the great army of veterans held captives in Northern prisons, was earnest and universal; and this desire for speedy and continuous exchange on the part of the government, as well as on the part of the people, sprang not merely from motives of compassion for their unfortunate kindred and fellow-soldiers, but also from the dictates of that policy, which would exchange on the part of a weak and struggling people, a large army of prisoners (consumers and non-combatants, requiring an army for their safe-keeping), for an army of tried veterans.

Apart from the real facts of the case, it is impossible to conceive that any government, in the distressed and struggling state of the Confederate States, could deliberately advocate any policy which would deprive it of a large army of veterans, and compel it to waste its scant supplies, already insufficient for the support of its struggling and retreating armies.

And the result has shown that the destruction of the Confederate Government was accomplished as much by the persistent retention in captivity of the Confederate soldiers, as by the emancipation and arming of the Southern slaves, and the employment of European recruits.

And still farther to show that these accidents attending vaccination at Andersonville were active in Northern prisons, we quote the testimony of a medical officer who occupied during the war a distinguished position in the Medical Department of the United States Army.

Dr. Frank Hastings Hamilton, late Lieutenant-Colonel, Medical Inspector, U. S. A., in his "Treatise on Military Surgery," records the following facts which have an important bearing upon the subject under consideration:

"In still further confirmation of the correctness of our views, we will mention that in many of the regiments stationed in Kentucky and Tennessee during the summer of 1863, all slight wounds, such as scratches, slight burns, etc., took on an ulcerative action and often became ugly and intractable sores. Vaccination almost constantly produced the same results, and was in many cases followed by abscesses in the axillary, cervical, and other glands.

"Upon the evacuation of Murfreesboro by the Confederate Army, on the first of January, 1863, 1673 sick and wounded soldiers were left in our hands; of these 250 were sick, and 1423 were wounded. The whole number were placed in chage of Dr. Avent, the intelligent Medical Director of General Bragg's army, assisted by several other Confederate Surgeons, and were allowed to remain in the buildings which they had originally taken as hospitals, and which were the best the place afforded. On the 20th of May, 1863, nearly five months after the battle of Stone's River (Murfreesboro), Dr. Avent reported to us that 640 of these men had died, and 55 remained in the hospital, the remainder having been sent off for exchange. The ratio of deaths, continues Dr. Avent, allowing the same percentage for the 55 now on hand, is about $38\frac{1}{4}$ per cent. I have not seperated the sick in this calculation from the wounded, from the fact that the hospitals were common to both; consequently I have no positive data on which to make an estimate of the relative mortality. I am satisfied, however, that the mortality amongst the sick has been much less than of the wounded. An estimate, placing the percentage of the wounded at about 40, I think would not be far wrong; which loss, you will discvover, is unprecedented in any previous battle between the present belligerents.

"In explanation of this great mortality after wounds, Dr. Avent proceeds to offer several facts; namely, over-crowding of the patients in the hospital buildings, mental depression, the fact that only the most severely wounded were left behind; but he gives especial prominence to the physical condition of the men, in consequence of a prolonged absence in their food of anti-scorbutic articles, both before and since their capture."

We have here a far heavier mortality amongst these Confederate Prisoners, than amongst the Andersonville Prisoners; and according to the published statements of the United State Government the majority of deaths during the war was largely on the side of the Confederate Soldiers confined in Northern Prisons. And after careful inquiries amongst returned Confederate prisoners, I am convinced that the accidents attending vaccination were quite as numerous and severe in Northern Prisons as in Southern; and the causes of death amongst prisoners in both sections were not materially different, with this exception, that the heat of the Southern States was balanced by the effects of severe cold upon feeble scorbutic men with insufficient clothing.

We have dwelt thus long upon this subject, because we have considered its discussion, of paramount interest, in the history of vaccination, and of the Profession in America.

In many cases occuring in the Confederate Army, the deleterious effects of vaccination, were clearly referable to the condition of the forces, and the constitution of the blood of the patients, for it was observed in a number of instances that the same lymph from a healthy infant, inoculated upon different individuals, produced results corresponding to the state of the system; in those who were well fed and robust, producing no ill effects, whilst in the soldiers who had been subjected to incessant fatigue, exposure and poor diet, the gravest results followed.

The history of vaccination in the Army of Virginia under General Lee was of great interest, in the light which it threw upon these questions, and it is with deep regret that we learn that all the most valuable field reports were destroyed.

The following letter from Dr. L. Guild, formerly Medical Director of the Army of Northern Virginia (General Lee's Army), was received in reply to my request, for the experience upon this subject, of this surgeon, who had held one of the most responsible and distinguished positions in the Medical Department of the Confederate Army.

MOBILE, ALA., 12th Dec., 1866.

PROFESSOR JOSEPH JONES—*Dear Sir:*—Your letter of the 5th inst., has been received.

It would afford me great pleasure to contribute to your contemplated monograph on "Spurious Vaccination;" but in the retreat of the Army of Northern Virginia from Petersburg to Appomattox Court-House, all of the retained papers, professional notes, reports, &c., of my office were either destroyed by the enemy or burned, with other baggage, by our own people for the purpose of lightening our trains and facilitating the movement of our retreating columns. When the boxes were burned their contents were, of course, unknown to those entrusted with the execution of the order. On account of this misfortune, I have nothing with which to refresh my memory accurately, in a single case, out of the vast number that came under my observation.

The subject of the transmission of syphilis through the vaccine virus is a most interesting and important one to the profession—admitting great diversity of opinion, and, as you truthfully remark, " one well-reported case is worth volumes of mere opinions and assertions."

I know of no one who could report such a case, but much useful information on the subject can be furnished by Dr. R. J. Breekinrigde—now of Houston, Texas—formerly of Louisville, Ky. He was one of the Medical Inspectors of the Army of Northern Virginia, and it was his duty, on several occasions, to collect and collate all interesting facts and opinions on the subject, such as the nature and character of the ulcers following vaccination, anterior history of patients, effects of treatment constitutional and local, &c., &c.

I regret my inability to furnish something worthy of your consideration.

Respectfully, yours, &c., L. GUILD.

The testimony of Dr. S. E. Habersham, upon this cause of the abnormal phenomena accompanying and following vaccination, is clear and important.

The following Report, was placed in my hands by its author, and was accompanied with the following answer to my request and inquiries:

SUMMERVILLE. April 28th, 1866.

DR. JOSEPH JONES—*Dear Sir:*—The accompanying report of an anomalous disease or result of vaccination, was written shortly after its first appearance in the Army of Northern Virginia, and after a careful study of the cases especially assigned to the Hospital under my charge for " treatment and report." At the time, there was much discussion among the Medical Staff, both in Field and Hospital, as to the ætiology and pathology of the manifestation which by some, and, indeed, most of the observers, was attributed to impure virus, and especially syphilitical inoculation. This latter opinion was ingeniously advocated by Surgeon Breekinridge, and no doubt many cases may have resulted from such an accident. In none of the cases, however, assigned to my Division of Chimborazo Hospital, could I discover a sufficient number of symptoms to lead me to suppose that such might have been the cause, either in its prodroma or development, hence I could not attribute the cause of the eruption to any other than that assigned in the report. This view as to its ætiology was subsequently very ably maintained by Surgeon Frank A. Ramsey, in a report referred to me by Surgeon-General Moore, and which was preserved among my papers, but lost at the time of the evacuation of Richmond, together with the history of all the cases, and diagrams intended to illustrate the above report. In consequence of the loss of these papers this report is not as perfect as it should be; but I hope the general description and history of the disease is sufficiently clear and comprehensive to embrace every thing of practical importance concerning this horribly disgusting and filthy accident, or result of vaccination, as seen in our army.

Since the termination of the war, I have had several opportunities of conversing with a few intelligent Surgeons of the Federal Army, and ascertained from them that such a disease had appeared among their soldiers in regions of country where the scorbutic diathesis manifested itself among the troops, and to which the disease was generally attributed by them, though there were also Surgeons of that army who attributed it to syphilitic inoculation. I find the same view as advanced in the accompanying report held by most of the Surgeons of the Federal Army, as stated in Circular No. 6, Surgeon-General's Office, U. S. Army, November 1, 1865.

If you think my report of sufficient importance to appear upon the pages of your journal, or if it can in any way advance the cause of medical knowledge, you are at perfect liberty to make use of it for that purpose.

With much respect, I remain,
Very truly, your obedient servant,

S. E. HABERSHAM.

Report on Spurious Vaccination in the Confederate Army By S. E. HABERSHAM, M.D., Surgeon in the Provisional Army of the Confederate States.

CHIMBORAZO HOSPITAL, DIV. No. 2, November, 1863.

To Surgeon W. A. CARRINGTON, *Medical Director*—

SIR: I have the honor to inform you that, in accordance with your order of the 29th June, 1863, I have received all the patients sent into this Division, with a "peculiar eruptive disease," supposed to be the consequence of vaccination, and herewith forward you the results of my investigation into this anomalous affection.

In compliance with an order issued from the Surgeon-General's Office in the month of November, 1862, general vaccination was practiced upon all soldiers as soon as they were admitted into this Division, and in order to insure the full protective influence of vaccination (not anticipating any evil consequences therefrom), the order was strictly obeyed, and all the patients, even those having recent scars upon them, were re-vaccinated. A few days after the insertion of the virus, and, in many cases, within twenty-four hours, the seat of puncture became very much inflamed, with a deep inflammatory blush around it, which gradually implicated, in the severe cases, nearly the whole of the affected limb. A pustule rapidly formed, instead of a vesicle, which very soon discharged an ichorous fluid. This fluid was, in the course of forty-eight hours, converted into a dark, mahogany-colored, irregularly-shaped scab, prominent, and firmly attached at its base. A dark-red areola of several lines in diameter, measuring from the edge of the scab, was then developed, which, in turn, seemed to exude an ichorous serum. This was soon converted into a scab surrounding in juxtaposition the first, and presenting the appearance of a single scab. This process continued for several days, and there was often formed a scab, one inch or two and a half in diameter. "Pari passu" with the increase of this scab, the erysipelatous blush on the limb diminished, and when the blush had disappeared, this scab ceased to enlarge. As this inflammatory process subsided, the discharge lost its serous character, and seemed to be converted into pus, which exuded from under the scab, loosening its firm attachment at its base, and thus rendering it liable to be removed prematurely by the patient in his sleep, or even by the friction of his clothing. When this occurred, a foul bleeding, irregularly shaped phagedenic ulcer was revealed, with everted edges, and presenting the appearance of a Syphilitic phagedenic ulcer, involving the subcutaneous areola tissue, exposing, in many cases, the muscular tissue below. The process of destruction of parts did not end here, for the ulcer continued to increase, and from the loosened edges an ichorous discharge continued to pour out from under the skin which seemed to destroy the edges of the ulcer, thus increasing its dimensions. Wherever the ichorous pus from this ulcer touched the sound skin, another pustule of a similar character was formed, in some cases reaching the size of the primary sore. This, however, was seldom the case, but a smaller ulcer generally resulted, which often healed and cicatrized before the first.

The Axillary Glands, when the arm was affected, and the Inguinal Glands, when the leg was the seat of the disease, sometimes became inflamed and discharged pus, presenting the microscopic character of healthy pus. This enlargement of glands, however, did not occur in a sufficient number of cases to make it a natural sequence of the disease. Attending the early stages of the formation of the ulcer, before pus was discharged, there was always more or less pyrexia, with furred tongue and loss of appetite; these symptoms disappearing as soon as ulceration was established. In these highly aggravated cases, successive crops of pustules made their appearance on the affected limb, often developing themselves also upon the lower limbs of the affected side, but seldom crossing the mesian line, and never developing themselves upon the trunk or head.

The less malignant form of the disease resembled the first in character, but not in degree. For a few days after the insertion of the virus, merely a small inflamed spot was discerned, which seemed to be more the result of the injury done to the skin, by the prick of the lancet, than any inflammatory action resulting from a specific cause. About the fifth or sixth day a minute pustule was discerned upon a scarcely larger inflamed base. This pustule and areola gradually increased, but the diameter of the areola was not as great, and there was no deep inflammatory blush upon the arm, merely a diffused redness of several inches in diameter. The same process, however, took place—an exudation of serum from the areola—which, in turn, became a crust, and which gradually increased in size; but it never reached the diameter of the more malignant type; and when it was detached by the process of ulceration, which occurred at an early period, the revealed ulcer was neither as deep nor as malignant in its appearance. The edges were not everted, and there was no discharge of pus from under the edges of the ulcer; it only presented the appearance of an ordinary ulcer, showing no tendency to increase, and but little to heal. Pyrexia very seldom attended this form, nor was the appetite impaired.

The third and mildest form of the disease made its appearance as a small pimple, in from two to ten days after the introduction of the virus, and which gradually formed a pustule; a dark brown scab succeeded in from three to four days, which remained attached sometimes as long as two weeks, and when it become detached, a livid or brown spot was revealed, the size of which was equal to the scab. This scar, however, was very sensitive to the touch, and liable to bleed from the least friction of clothing, and when this occurred, it would exude serum or blood, and another scab would surely form. If the system became suddenly depressed from any cause, it would almost always assume the ulcerative process, and become a sloughing ulcer, which only healed with the general improvement of the system.

As thus described, this disease has prevailed in the Army of Virginia, both in field and hospital. The Surgeons of the Army of the Southwest, report its prevalence there. It was developed, in the early part of the year, in a Cavalry Regiment in the mountains of Virginia, the Colonel commanding suffering severely from the disease. In every case, its origin has been traced to the introduction of vaccine virus into the system. How far an epidemic cause may have exerted its influence in its early development, it is impossible even to surmise; we know, however, that it originated in Virginia, at a time when our Army was upon very short rations, and that many of the soldiers sent from the field at that time presented a decidedly scorbutic appearance. Many had been reduced and were broken down by exposure to the inclemency of a cold winter, and the depressing influences of low diet, want of clothing, and many other prolific causes of disease, calculated to deprive the blood of its healthy constituents, particularly of its fatty matter. Hence this may have produced a predisposition. In verification of this fact, I will state, that when it was found how frequently the disease in consideration supervened upon Vaccination in this hospital in broken-down and depraved constitutions, it was deemed prudent to postpone the introduction of the virus until the patient was restored to a healthy condition by improved diet and medical treatment. At the first appearance of the evil consequences of Vaccination, I was inclined, with other Surgeons, to believe that the virus was impure, and, because of this suspicion, I threw away the matter we then had, and obtained a vaccine scab from Dr. Knox a practitioner on Church Hill, who assured me he had used it in several cases with a perfect result.

The introduction of this virus into the arms of some ten patients resulted in the development of the disease in question in three of them, while in the remainder it produced apparently a true pustule. From this fact, and the immunity which healthy looking men enjoyed, I was led to believe that the predisposing cause existed in a vitiated and impoverished condition of the blood, and so reported in my first report, and that the introduction of pure virus into the system was the exciting cause of a latent disease. This view, I see, is also held by Surgeon Frank A. Ramsey, of the Department of East Tennessee, in a communication on file in office of Surgeon General. This view I have never had reason to change, though I am aware that many men, apparently in health, have suffered from the effects of Vaccination.

In one case, which I here quote, the influence of a good condition of the general system seems to have exerted a wonderfully modifying influence.

Case No. 29.—J. L. Turner, a private, Company G, fifth Virginia Cavalry, aged 27, married, parents healthy—he himself enjoying good health—never had any venereal disease. Entered the service, April, 1861—has been in service ever since, was vaccinated about a month ago, when in Hospital at Farmville.

This patient, Turner, was vaccinated last winter by Assistant Surgeon Vaiden, of this Division. It not having any effect upon his system, and feeling assured from this and previous Vaccinations that he was proof against the effect of it, he insisted upon being vaccinated by Assistant Surgeon Moses, from the effects of which he has suffered since, and for which he was on the 8th September admitted to this Hospital, presenting the following appearance: A number of pustules, resembling Impetigo, on left arm and leg, which were developed in successive crops, appearing as soon as the original pustule began to heal. This was a remarkably mild form of the disease, and was improving on Cod Liver Oil, when he was furloughed on the 20th September, being a paroled prisoner. This patient was young, vigorous, and comparatively healthy, when he received this Vaccine into his system.

The search, for parasitic or cryptogamic vegetation, with a good microscope revealed none. The pustule was seldom developed where Parasites make their habit tation, namely, in the bulbs, or at the roots of the hair. The pus presented microscopic characteristics of pus globules floating in a homogenous fluid. These globules were not as abundant as in laudable pus, and not so distinctly nucleated, and were irregular in outline in some of the cases examined. This appearance of globules, however, often exists in healthy or laudable pus, when it has been exposed to air any length of time. In the many cases I have examined, I have yet to find a patient who will acknowledge that he has had any Syphilitic disease at any period of his life, though many of them have had Gonorrhœa. This exemption from Syphilis, however, is not strange, since it is a very uncommon disease in the rural parts of our country, the inhabitants of which comprise the very large majority of our Army. We also know that the tendency of the secondary form of Syphilis is to develope itself in the forehead, chest, back, and trunk, generally, and yet no cases, developed upon these parts of the body, have presented themselves to my observation. Many of the patients, also, have suffered long enough to have had the tertiary form of Syphilis developed nodes, etc., and yet no such symptoms have been seen by me.

From what I can learn, the Army of the United States has so far escaped these evil results of Vaccination. A few cases, however, originated among the Federal, officers, in the Hospital of Libby Prison, who were vaccinated in the Prison by one of their Surgeons from his own arm, some weeks after their confluement, which presented all the characteristics of the disease as it has appeared in our Army. I was assured by these officers that they had neither seen or heard of such a result of Vaccination in their Army. Does not this fact alone lead us to infer that its cause of origin may be traced to some abnormal condition of the blood, in these cases, induced by confinement in a vitiated atmosphere, without the means of eliminating the *materies morbi* from the system by exercise, and care to the function of the skin.

The classification of this disease is difficult and unsatisfactory, since it commences as a Pustule, and assumes often the outward form of Rupia, which, by all dermatologists is classified among the bullae. If we classify it among the pustulæ, we find no diesease there describing it accurately, some cases resembling Ecthyma, others Impetigo. Inasmuch, however, as it oftener assumes the characteristics of Chronic Ecthyma, either in a mild or aggravated form, according to the healthy or unhealthy condition of the patient, I propose to name it Vaccine Ecthyma. Like all chronic cutaneous diseases, it shows a decided tendency to return whenever the system becomes reduced from any cause, or when the patient is exposed to causes which produce an undue action in the circulation of the capillary system. An undue amount of exercise in warm weather seems to excite its appearance. This was illustrated in those soldiers supposed to be thoroughly cured, and who were about to be ordered to their Regiments for duty, when a raid was threatened, in the month of July, upon the City of Richmond. These men were among the volunteers from the hospital to defend the city, and were marched through a hot sun some four miles to the lines at the extreme limits of the western end of the town. They returned with a new crop of pustules, which, however, healed by resolution in a short time.

Treatment.—There is every reason to believe that the disease results from a blood disease, only to be eliminated from the system by enriching the blood and supplying its deficiency of fatty matter with rich nutritious food and by the judicious use of alteratives. It is in vain to treat the ulcers locally, for without alterative treatment with nutritious diet, all the local applications which were tried seemed to aggravate rather than improve them; but as soon as the general condition began to improve, so did the ulcers. The milder cases began to improve a few weeks after admission without any treatment, except dietetic, in conjunction with the Iodide of Potash, Syrup Iod. Ferri, and Sarsaparilla; in others, merely applying simple dressing to the ulcers, was found sufficient to subdue it. Under this treatment, all the cases gradually but slowly improved. In the early part of August, we received a large supply of Cod Liver Oil, and I was thus enabled to test fully the treatment which the supposed cause of the disease naturally suggested. Some few of the patients could not digest the Oil, but those who could began rapidly to improve, and many were able to return to their Regiments, whilst others were thought well enough to be transferred to their respective State Hospitals, in compliance with an order issued at that time. Those who were unable to digest the Oil, continued the Syrup Iod. Ferri, which was thought the best alterative indicated in their cases. Their improvement was scarcely perceptible. In the early part of September, however, another effort was made by them to take the Cod Liver Oil which they were enabled to do in a little Whisky; their improvement soon became very evident to themselves and though not entirely well, the ulcers are rapidly granulating, No new pustules are being developed, and the patients are in a fair way to recover. I have no doub that the best remedy has been found in the Cod Liver Oil; and this, locally applied and internally administered, with an entire change of air and nutritious diet, will remove, and eventually eradicate, this obnoxious and filthy disease from the system.

From the above mentioned facts, I am led to draw the following conclusions: That the disease is pustular at its first appearance; that it resembles Ecthyma in its general character; that it is but a local manifestation of a general disorder, or vitiated condition of the blood; that this vitiated condition resulted from improper and spare diet, together with inattention to cleanliness, thus impairing the eliminating functions of the skin; that Syphilitic virus has had no influence in producing the disease; that the morbid effects have in most of the cases resulted from deficiency in condition, independent of any imperfection in the Vaccine Virus; that the disease can only be removed by those means caluclated to improve the general condition and restore the healthy play of all the functions.

SECTION III.

THE EMPLOYMENT OF MATTER, FROM PUSTULES OR ULCERS WHICH HAD DEVIATED FROM THE REGULAR AND NORMAL COURSE OF DEVELOPMENT OF THE VACCINE VESICLE; SUCH DEVIATION OR IMPERFECTION IN THE VACCINE DISEASE AND PUSTULE, BEING DUE MAINLY TO PREVIOUS VACCINATION, AND THE EXISTENCE OF SOME ERUPTIVE DISEASE AT THE TIME OF VACCINATION. OR, IN OTHER WORDS, THE EMPLOYMENT OF

Matter from patients who had been previously Vaccinated, and who were partially protected, or who were affected with some Skin Disease at the time of the insertion of the Vaccine Virus.

Whilst it might admit of debate, whether pure vaccine virus' obtained from persons never before vaccinated, and who manifested all the phenomena of the disease, and especially the characteristic febrile phenomena, ever becomes deteriorated or possessed of deleterious properties in its passage through numerous human bodies, not suffering with such a contagious disease as syphilis; on the other hand, it cannot be denied that the protective power of vaccination has been impaired to a lamentable and almost incalculable extent, by a succession of imperfect vaccinations; and especially by the employment of matter from those who have been previously vaccinated, or who have suffered from small-pox previous to vaccination.

Vaccination may be rendered imperfect by the development of febrile and other diseased states after the introduction of the virus into the system, arising from the action of cold, or some cause producing constitutional disturbances differing essentially from the febrile phenomena which mark the progress and perfection of the vaccine disease; as well as by its imperfect and altered course in those who are partially protected by previous vaccination.

In the isolated condition of the Southern Confederacy, cut off from the surrounding world, and denied even vaccine matter, as "*contraband of war;*" with the necessity of turning out the entire fighting population to repel invasion, and with the necessity of employing all the available medical aid, good, bad, and indifferent; and with the progressive increase of small-pox; it is not strange that the process of vaccination was not as carefully watched and tested as it should have been: and that consequently much imperfect material circulated as *vaccine matter*, which not only afforded little or no protection against small-pox, but also proved positively deleterious.

My friend and colleague, Professor Paul F. Eve, M.D., of the University of Nashville, has recorded in his discussion of certain questions relative to the health of the late Southern Army, interesting observations upon Spurious Vaccination; and it will be seen, from the following extracts, that this distinguished surgeon, inclines to the belief, that the abnormal manifestations of the vaccine disease, may be due, in a great measure, to the alteration of the matter in consequence of its passing through a long succession of human subjects, and in consequence of the co-existence of various diseases.

"The scab used in Atlanta, which did so much mischief, was soft, porous, and spongy, of a yellowish brown color, resembling concrete, inspissated pus. It was not a small, hard, compact, translucent substance, like dried compressed glue, of dark mahogany color, requiring, as the genuine scab does, considerable effort to break it; neither did it present the clear, even, vitreous aspect when fractured, but was bulky, irregular and crumbling. In every instance, wherein vaccination was attempted with it, premature effects were developed. No proper period of incubation, nor papular or vesicular eruption was observed, but in a few days, even as early as the second, inflammation had set up, and by the fourth or fifth day, sores were produced, covered by a thick, dirty crust, with an ichorous discharge. Soon an ill-constituted ulcer, with perpendicular edges, ensued, extending through the dermoid to the cellular and muscular tissues, and involving the neighboring lymphatics. The cutaneous surface suffered chiefly, presenting large, irritable, very dark colored and scabby ulcers. Sometimes there was one, in other cases several, not on the extremity only into which the matter had been inserted, but on the others, and sometimes on the body. These cases were greatly aggravated by complications with erysipelas, scorbutus, syphilis, itch, etc. I believe we had no death from an uncomplicated case of Spurious Vaccination, though forty to fifty patients were treated in this hospital. * * While every deviation from the regular development of the vaccine disease may be considered spurious, we yet understand now by that term, a pretty well defined, certainly a peculiar, if not a specific affection, which we have already attempted to describe. * *

Intimately connected with the nature of spurious vaccination, is involved the question of its being simply a local affection, or constitutional disease. To what are its symptoms due; to a virus, or do they arise from cachexia? I am free to confess that the investigation of this subject has caused me to reverse the opinion, that the effects of impure vaccination are alone to be attributed to the bad condition of the patient's system, and did not depend upon anything special or specific. From repeated experiments, it is well ascertained that laudable pus when inserted into a healthy person is inocuous, and should it be used even in a decomposing or concrete state, will not excite certain uniform and peculiar results. Impure blood, peculiarity of constitution, indulgencies, epidemic influence, etc., etc., will account I know, for many local disturbances, but not for the origin of spurious vaccination. In every case it is the result of vaccination with impure virus, by careless or inexperienced persons. In reference to the nature of this impurity, there is good reason to believe that it results from a perversion or modification in the vaccine vesicle. We know heat destroys vaccine, as well as variolous virus, and it may be that excessive inflammatory action changes the genuine vaccine matter into the spurious. Or it may be this virus affected by another disease, or the bad state of the system, or becoming nearly effete itself, by passing through numerous systems produces a disease only resembling the true vaccine. The difficulty of developing genuine vaccination in one once impressed by the spurious, shows plainly the connection between the two."—*The Nashville Journal of Medicine and Surgery*, New Series. Vol. 1. 1866. pp. 21-28.

It will be seen from the following interesting communication, that Doctor Hamilton, of Chattanooga, who enjoyed ample opportunities for the investigation of the accidents following vaccination in the Confederate Army, attributes much of the spurious vaccination, to the careless use of matter from imperfect vesicles or sores.

CHATTANOOGA, Jan., 15, 1866.

PROF. JOSEPH JONES: DEAR SIR:—Your note of the 5th was received some time since. Sickness, absence from home, and professional duties have prevented an earlier reply, which I much regret, but cannot remedy.

In regard to the subjects named, I fear I can afford but little information worthy of your consideration.

Of what is termed "Spurious Vaccination," I saw many instances during my service as Surgeon in the army; and while in charge of the General Hospital at Strawberry Plains, East Tennessee, I was directed, from the Surgeon General's Office, to make a statistical report of all cases which had come to my knowledge. In obedience to this order, I had collected notes of many cases, but shortly after came the evacuation of East Tennessee, and my engagement in a different field of labor, so that the report was not made, and most of the notes which I had accumulated were "lost or destroyed by unavoidable accident."

From the few notes I have on hand, and from such facts as I can recall to memory, I give you herewith the general results.

All the cases, with a few exceptions, of "Spurious Vaccination," which came under my observation during the war, were reducible to one of the three following named classes:

1st. A single suppurating ulcer at the point of vaccination.

2d. General eruptions, sometimes single, sometimes in patches involving a considerable extent of surface, appearing during the existence of the original ulcer, or after it had healed.

3d. General eruptions attended by suppuration of the lymphatic glands.

To what extent these different forms may be regarded as seperate stages of the same development, I am not prepared to say, and I believe that no connection exists between them in such a sense. There certainly was no discoverable progression through the different conditions, such as is seen in some diseases.

It is evident that the result of any vaccination or inoculation must depend upon one or both of the following causes:

1st. Upon the kind of virus used.

2d. Upon the condition of the patient.

If vaccine virus is not used in any particular instance the result will be useless and perhaps hurtful to the patient. I am forced to the conclusion that a large majority of the cases of "Spurious Vaccination," which came under my observation during the war, were such because of the spuriousness of the virus used. If, by supposed vaccination, a "sore" was produced on the arm, the virus was supposed to be "taking," and straightway the matter was put into other arms, and other "sores" produced, when, on examination it would be found that not one of the arms gave evidence of vaccination. The pustules did not possess the characteristics of true vaccine, either in their progress or in their results. The proper scar was not left by them, nor the usual protection from variola afforded. A portion of liquid or encrusted pus, or of epithelium, was inserted in the arm, and the patient was presumed to be vaccinated. In some instances true vaccine virus was used on persons whose systems were protected by previous vaccination, and the matter from the resulting pustules, when used with others, became a source of evil. Soldiers practiced upon themselves from the arm of one of their number, whence came a long train of evil results.

But there were instances where portions of the same scab, produced in some persons the true vaccine pustule, and in others only the spurious eruption, and the explanation must be found in the condition of the patient. Just what this peculiar condition is, or what its causes are, we know not. The questions concerning the influence of army life on the physical, mental and moral condition of men recently taken from the walks of civil life, are many and various, and as yet, I believe most of us are only "guessing" at answers. Every medical officer remembers how fatal among soldiers, at times, were complaints which are ordinarily remediable, and that too, when, at the time of the appearance of the disease, the soldiers were apparently in robust health. It will also be remembered how very few instances occurred of what would be regarded as types of any one disease, while at the same time a large number of cases would be found. Nearly all were more or less modified, and some so completely as almost to lose their identity. But this subject is too extensive for discussion at this time.

In regard to the transmission of syphilitic poison through the process of vaccination, I can recall to mind a few instances, where I feel positively certain that secondary syphilitic eruptions existed, and the patients were equally positive in their expressed belief that the symptoms came from vaccination. Such cases were always diagnosticated as syphilitic, and treated and relieved as such My experience leads me to put so little faith in the assertions of persons affected with any venereal disease, on this subject, that I have arrived at no reasonable conclusion, and I can only say with the poet—begging pardon for so unpoetic a connection—"Though I canna see, I guess and fear."

To sum up then, in a few words. First—It is my belief that most of the cases of so-called spurious vaccination resulted from the fact that vaccine virus was not used, and therefore no vaccination, in the proper sense of the term took place. Secondly—The condition of the system, affected by atmospheric influence, or the kind of life led by soldiers, or by what you will, so modified the action of the virus as to produce morbid results.

I regret that circumstances prevent a more extended consideration of the subject touched on in this letter, such as their importance demands, and I rejoice to learn that you are preparing a Monograph on the same, and I shall look forward with much interest for its appearance in print.

Very truly yours, R. D. HAMILTON.

Dr. Jenner in the beginning of his inquiries, felt the propriety of watchfulness ; and at an early day he distinctly announced that it was possible to propagate an affection by vaccination conveying different degrees of security, according as that affection approached to, or receded from, the full and perfect standard ; he also clearly stated that the course of the vaccine pustule might be so modified as to deprive it of its efficacy, and that inoculation from such a source might communicate an inefficient protection, and that all who were thus vaccinated were more or less liable to subsequent small-pox. He still farther maintained that fluid taken from a genuine pustule in its far advanced stages, is capable of producing varieties which will be permanent if we continue to employ it. Dr. Jenner attached great importance to the condition of the skin at the time of the insertion of the virus.

In his tract "On the Varieties and Modifications, of the Vaccine Pustule occasioned by an herpetic state of the skin," he says, "I shall here just observe, that the most careful testimonies now lie before me supporting my opinion that the herpetic, and some other irritative eruptions, are capable of rendering variolous inoculation imperfect, as well as the vaccine."

One of the entries in his Journal is to the following effect : "Inoculated Lady C. F. a second time. It is very evident that *that* affection of the skin called red-gum, deadens the effect of the vaccine virus. This infant was covered with it when inoculated four days ago. The same thing happened to Mrs. D's. infant."

In a letter to Mr. Dunning, dated Berkely, Dec. 23, 1804 Dr. Jenner says :

"There may be peculiarities of constitution favorable to this phenomnon. My opinion still is, that the grand interference is from the agency of the herpes, in some form or another ; for I have discoverd that it is very Proteus, assuming, as it thinks fit, the character of the greater part of the irritative eruptions that assail us. I shall have much to say on this disease one of these days."

The reported failures of vaccination, and the occurence of several violent variolous epidemics in different parts of the country, induced him to endeavor to rouse the attention of professional men to those points, in the practice of vaccination which he deemed essential to its success. With such intentions he printed a circular letter early in 1821, which was sent to most of the respectable medical men in England; in it he directed their observation to the three following questions :—

"First. Whether the vaccine vesicle goes through its course with the same regularity when the skin is under the influence of any herpetic or eruptive disease, as when it is free from such affections; secondly, whether the existence of such eruptive diseases causes any resistance to the due action of vaccine lymph, when inserted into the arms; thirdly, whether cases of smallpox, after vaccination had occurred to the observer; and if so, whether such occurrences could be ascribed to any deviation in the progress of the vaccine pustule, in consequence of the existence of herpetic, or other eruptions, at the time of vaccination."—*The Life of Edward Jenner, M.D.*, LL.D., F.R.S., &c., by John Baron, M.D., vol. ii. p. 272.

The answer to these inquiries, by the Rector of Leckhamstead, contains facts of such value in their bearing upon this portion of the subject, that we are induced to reproduce it entire:

LECKHAMSTEAD, NEAR BUCKINGHAM, June 29th, 1820.

EDWARD JENNER, M.D.: *Dear Sir:*—Your letter did not reach Buckingham till June 23rd, though dated the 12th. The object of inquiry appears to be the extent to which cutaneous diseases reject or modify the vaccine virus, so as to render the efficacy and security doubtful. I have looked over a number of copies of communications to Dr. Harvey, and will with great pleasure send you the transcripts of the interference of variolus and vaccine infection, and the superseding power of the latter if applied in time, six of which took place at Old Stratford in 1816, among the children of one family, being the whole time under the same roof. The distress and alarm at that time were extremely great, as the inhabitants were recovering from the measles when the small-pox broke out. The anxiety of the parents was such that I was induced, contrary to my own opinion, to vaccinate several where the fever of measles had not completely subsided: the consequence of which was nothing more than that the vaccine virus lay dormant in its cell till the field was clear, and came into action two or three days later; but afterwards proceeded in as regular and decided a manner as in constitutions which were not previously engaged.

I discovered at a very early period that the itch was not an impediment; as to the shingles, I cannot speak. The grand rejecting agent in children is the tooth rash, or, as it is here commonly called, the red gum, especially while it continues bright and active. Dr. William Cleaver (when Bishop of Chester) promoted an extensive variolous inoculation in his diocese. Some years after, he asked me if I could account for the very frequent failure of communicating the infection to young children. I told him that it applied equally to the vaccine; though frequently, if the virus was fresh and active, it would be suspended in its career for a time only, but push forward with success at last.

I beg to assure you, Sir, that nothing I have met with has, in the slightest degree, shaken my faith in the vaccine. I have seven children, the eldest sixteen, all vaccinated by myself; and of 14,305, all within a few miles of this place, I have never heard of a single fatal disappointment; and of only two or three cases of modified, or what I should feel inclined to call superficial, or cutaneous small-pox. As to remote or derivative diseases, I know of no such thing fairly to be ascribed to the cow-pox; I have ample means of knowing if such a thing had taken place, as the people of my two parishes, and many in the neighborhood, are, somehow or other, continually coming under my consideration for medical assistance. My communications of late years have been to Dr. Harvey according to the directions of the National Establishment; but I have met with no demand for inoculation since February' 1820, simply from the absence of any stimulating alarm.

I am dear Sir, with the highest respect,
Your most obedient humble servant,
T. T. A. REED, Rector of Leckhamstead.

Mr. Reed had, in 1806, printed and distributed a tract for the encouragement of those who entertained any doubt respecting the efficacy of vaccine inoculation; and distinguished himself as an ardent and successful promoter of vaccination; his testimony, therefore, is of great value.

Dr. Jenner maintained to the last hour of his life, that any cutaneous disease, however slight in appearance, was capable of interfering with the regular course of the cow-pox, and of preventing it from exercising its full protecting influence: and his directions for obviating any deterioration of the virus, regarded first, the character of the pustule itself, the time and quality of the lymph taken for inoculation, and all other circumstances that might go to affect the complete progress of the disorder. Thus he maintained that the vaccine fluid should be taken, for the purpose of inoeculation, at an early period of the formation of the vesicle, and before the appearance of the areola ; and he insisted that the pustule, when excited, should be permitted to go through all its stages in an uninterrupted manner, and if any deviations appeared in its progress, he always forbade the employment of virus from such a pustule for further vaccinations.

Dr. Waterhouse, in a letter to Dr. Mitchell, dated Cambridge, Sept. 26th, 1801, says : " Yesterday I received a letter from Dr. Jenner, one paragraph of which I must transcribe, because it contains the *golden rule of vaccination*, viz.: 'I don't care what British laws the Americans discard, so that they stick to this—*never to take the virus from a vaccine pustule for the purpose of inoculation, after the efflorescence is formed around it.* I wish this effloresence to be considered as a sacred boundary, over which the lancet should never pass.' "—*Med. Repository, N. Y.*, vol. v., p. 236.

Every deviation, from whatever cause it may have arisen, was considered by Jenner of the greatest moment ; and as has been fully shown by the learned author of his life, in all his published works, as well as in every private communication, he never failed to express his deep sense of the importance of the most scrupulous attention to that part of the subject ; and to the last he felt that, had his admonitions been received as they ought, had the phenomena connected with vaccine inoculation, been studied by all who conducted the practice, a large proportion of the failures would have been avoided.

The following important and interesting communication, published about forty-five years ago, confirms, in a striking manner, the correctness and great value of the laws laid down by Jenner, with reference to the relations of the vaccine disease to cutaneous affections :

OBSERVATIONS ON THE VACCINE AND VARIOLOID DISEASES. COMMUNICATED BY JAMES DAVIS, M.D., OF COLUMBIA, SOUTH CAROLINA.

I offer you the following communication, not only because it seems to corroborate the observations of Dr. Jenner and others, that the simultaneous existence of cutaneous diseases, with the vaccine pox, has a tendency to vitiate the virus of the latter disease, and render it unfit for communicating the true kine pock; but, moreover, because it would appear that the vaccine matter is liable, from this circumstance, to be converted into a virus of a totally different character.   *   *   *

I extract the following case from my note book:

On the 29th of June, 1814, I vaccinated Master James D. Montgomery, æt. 18 months, son of Dr. B. R. Montgomery, Professor of Moral Philosophy, &c., in the South Carolina College, together with six other healthy children. I had obtained the matter that I made use of from Dr. Smith of Baltimore. James D. Montgomery had been laboring under a cutaneous disease (the strophulus interlictus of Willan) for about three months. It had resisted every remedy which I had prescribed for it, and by this time had literally spread over the whole surface, so as to render it difficult to find a sound spot on the arm, large enough for making the insertion. I should have been deterred from vaccinating in such a case, but for a remark of Dr. Jenner, viz.: "That vaccination, although not very certain to take in cases of cutaneous eruption, yet, when it did take, it was curative of the cutaneous disorder." Upon this information, I recommended it to Dr. Montgomery, who readily acceded to the experiment. The vaccine failed to take effect in every one of the cases, except in that of J. D. Montgomery; and in his case, it was really gratifying and delightful to observe the effect of it on the cutaneous disease. As the vaccine pock advanced, the affection of the skin disappeared, and that in a very exact proportion to each other; so that, by the time the pock was mature, the cutaneous disorder had entirely gone off. From fifteen to twenty-five days after the kine-pock had been in its full course, he was afflicted with two abscesses, one on his back, and one on his breast, which discharged from half an ounce to an ounce of laudable pus; since which time he has remained in sound and perfect health.

His pock proved to be anomalous, and whether it were sufficient to protect his system against the small-pox has not since been tested. But from the constitutional symptoms which I attentively observed, I am very much inclined to believe, that as to himself, it was effectual.

The virus manifested no signs of having taken effect until the eighth day, when the small inflamed point at the puncture first appeared.

The areola did not progress from day to day with regularity, nor was it at any time sufficiently circumscribed, having some radii considerably longer than others. Its color was a coarse red, instead of that beautiful fine blush, which the genuine vaccine generally exhibits.

The pock, although of ordinary size, and of a concave surface, was destitute of that cordon of bead-like vesicles, which form around the corona of the true kine-pock. It was peculiarly dry, insomuch that it was difficult to obtain from it as much lymph as would serve for further vaccination.

Four healthy children (white and black) of the family of Dr. E. D. Smith, Professor of Chemistry, &c., were vaccinated from this pustule. I had expressed an opinion, that although I believed the constitution of little Master Montgomery was secured against the Small-pox, that, nevertheless, I doubted of the efficacy of the matter of his pustule to communicate the true disease. As matter, however, was hard to be obtained, and as it was conceived no danger could result from it, the Doctor determined on making the trial. It failed to produce any effect whatever on all, except on one of the Doctor's own children. In this case the puncture began to inflame within the first fourteen hours. The inflammation spread rapidly, accompanied with innumerable papulous eruptions over the inflamed suface, exuding a profuse quantity of gelatinous matter. It continued to spread for about thirty hours, assuming in its progress rather a formidable appearance, and exciting a good deal of alarm, until it occupied a space longer than five or six areolas of the true pock; extending over the one more longitudinally than laterally. Aperients were administered, and the topical affection fomented with a decoction of chamomile flowers, and in about forty-eight hours it had totally, disappeared, having exhibited no sign whatever of any thing like a pock. There was no constitutioal disturbance accompanying the affection. The child remained in perfect health, and has undergone the kinepock by a subsequent vaccination.

This case evinces two facts in a clear and decided manner, to wit: that the vaccine disease is capable of effecting the cure of certain inveterate diseases of the skin; and that certain diseases of the skin may exert such an influence over the vaccine matter, as not only to vitiate and render it unfit for communicating the true kinepock, but also absolutely to change and convert it into a poison of a new and unknown character. Two facts of great practical importance, and which perhaps, deserve more investigation and scrutiny, than they have hitherto received.

The influence of kine-pock over cutaneous disorders, is an old remark; and the influence of diseases of the skin in vitiating the matter of the kine pock, and rendering it unfit for communicating the true pock, is equally old. But its liability to be converted into a poison of a different nature, productive of singular and anomalous affections, in consequence of being blended with certain cutaneous disorders, is a subject which has not hitherto attracted as much attention as it merits. In this instance, the cutaneous disease of Master Montgomery, obviously occasioned a conversion of the vaccine matter into a new kind of virus, producing a new and singular affection. It is true, it proved to be a mere topical affection, and terminated without any serious consequences; but, as the vaccine matter is liable to be changed by one form of cutaneous disease, is it not reasonable to conclude, that it may also be changed by others? And although, in this particular case, it was changed into comparatively an inocuous virus, have we any evidence, that in blending with some others of the multifarious affections of the skin, incident to mankind, it may not become converted into a virus of deleterious and destructive operation?

All this however, indicates nothing against the utility and importance of *genuine* vaccination, but only shows how important it is that it should be practiced with a care, circumspection, and skill, with which the prevailing custom of our country at present is utterly incompatible; and until there shall be a reform effected in this respect, it will be in vain to look for the full extent of those beneficial results to mankind, which the kine-pock is unquestionably calculated to afford.

The attainment of these results in strict conformity with the laws of our condition in the attainment of every other great and important good, is beset with difficulties; nevertheless we have no reason to suppose that these difficulties are insuperable. Every year brings to light some new facts, which enable us to approach nearer and nearer to the attainment of the desired object. And as one principal obstacle to the improvement of our knowledge of this subject has been the apathy, indifference, and even levity with which it has been received by a great majority of the community; so, when, perhaps from severe afflictions and scourges, or from any other causes, this supineness and indifference shall be removed; then the marc of improvement will be rapidly accelerated, and great and permanent advantages will be the happy result.

Would it not be a wise precaution, and worthy of legislative provisions, to impose a penalty on any one who should communicate the vaccine disease from an unhealthy subject?—*The American Medical Recorder of Original Papers and Intelligence in Medicine and Surgery, conducted by John Eberle, M.D., Philadelphia, and H. W. Ducachet, M.D., New York, vol. v.*, 1822—pp. 268-272.

The power of the vaccine virus to relieve diseases of the skin, can only depend upon its absorption into the blood, and its effects upon the entire system : and facts are not wanting to show by actual manifestations of the local disease in other parts of the system not inoculated with the virus, that the entire system as well as the skin is brought under the action of this poison.

Dr. Denby, reported the case of Henry Freeman, a lad of twelve years of age, who was vaccinated in the left arm by the usual mode. The vesicle was marked by the appropiate progressive character of successful inoculation. It happened that on the same day on which he was vaccinated (five hours subsequent to that process,) an incised wound was accidentally inflicted on his right knee ; which wound, for two or three days promised union by the first intention. On the fourth or fifth day, however, an increase of pain was felt in the knee, with throbbing and heat about the edges of the wound ; and, on inspection, some slight papulae, to the number of ten or thirteen, were observed surrounding it. These appearances were yet referred to a common cause. On the eighth day, their peculiar and regular form imparted a conviction that they were true vaccine vesicles, which they proved to be by their progress and maturation.—*London Med. Press*, April, 1825.

As far as our knowledge extends, the records of Medicine, are singularly barren of critical observations upon the phenomena manifested by man, when acted upon, by two or more diseases at the same time. This imperfection of knowledge results not only from the complexity of the phenomena, and the difficulties of the investigation, but also from the comparatively infrequent occurrence of two or more contagious diseases, at the same time, in the same household, and in the same individual.

Every fact illustrating the relations of the vaccine disease, to other diieases arising simultaneously in the same individual, is of importance in the light which it throws upon the modifications of the vaccine disease, and upon the question of *the possibility of transmitting various contagious diseases through the medium of the vaccine virus.*

The following facts and observations by various writers, bearing upon these questions, which we have gathered up after some research, are presented under this division of our subject, to which they naturally belong, rather for the purpose of exciting and aiding farther investigation, than as full and complete investigations upon which definite and uncontrovertible principles may be founded. I have myself conducted extended investigations upon the mutual relations, of various concurrent diseases, as Malarial Fever, Typhoid Fever, Pneumonia, Cerebro-Spinal Meningitis, Hospital Gangrene and Pyæmia, the results of which it would be impossible to present at the present time, although related to the subject now under discussion ; and I shall present those facts which relate chiefly to the relations of Small Pox and the vaccine disease to several of ihe Exanthemata.

If we accept without reserve the doctrine of John Hunter, that "No two actions can take place in the same constitution or in the same part, at one and the same time : no two different fevers can exist in the same constitution, no two local diseases in the same part, at the same time ;" (*Works of John Hunter*, edited by James F, Palmer London 1837 vol. ii., Treatise on the venereal disease, p. 132): the question of the modification of the vaccine disease by concurrent diseases, as well as of the possibility of the transmission of contagious diseases through the medium of the vaccine virus is definitely settled in the negative. The unreserved assent to such a doctrine as this, is wholly incompatible with the admission of the possibilty of transmitting such a disease as Syphilis through the medium of the matter produced by a distinct disease, different in its mode of origin, constitutional action, symptoms and progress.

Even the renowned author of this doctrine, appears to have experienced difficulties, when he attempted to apply it universally. The engrafting of other diseases upon the systems of those who were laboring under constitutional syphilis, and scurvy, as well as the occasional occurence of these two diseased states in the same individual, presented at the outstep difficulties to the mind of John Hunter, which he attempted to remove by argument. The mode, as well as the facts, by which Hunter supported his doctrine are worthy of full consideration, in this connection, as gathered from various portions of his works.

"*Of diseased Actions, as being incompatible with each other.*—As I reckon every operation in the body an action, whether universal or partial, it appears to me beyond a doubt that no two actions can take place in the same constitution, nor in the same part, at one and the same time; the operations of the body are similar in this respect to actions or motions in common matter. It naturally results from this principle that no two different fevers can exist in the same constitution, nor two local diseases in the same part. There are many local diseases which have dispositions totally different, but, having very similar appearances, have been supposed by some to be one sort of disease, by others to be of a different kind, and by others again a compound of two diseases. Thus the venereal disease, when it attacks the skin, is very similar to those diseases which are vulgarly called scorbutic, and *vice versa*. These, therefore, are often supposed to be mixed, and to exist in the same part. Thus we hear of a pocky-scurvy, a pocky-itch, rheumatic-gout, &c., &c., which names, according to my principle imply a union that cannot possibly exist.

"It has been considered as contradictory to this opinion that a patient might have scrofula, scurvy, venereal disease, small-pox, &c., at the same time. All of this is indeed possible; but then no two of them can exist in the same part of the body at the same time; but before one of them can occupy the places of another, that other must be first destroyed, or it may be superseded for a time, and may afterwards return.

"When a constitution is susceptible of any one disease, this does not hinder it from being also susceptible of others. I can conceive it possible that a man may be very susceptible of every disease incident to the human body, although it is not probable; for I should believe that one susceptibility is in some degree incompatible with another, in a manner similar to the incompatibility between different actions, though not of so strict a kind.

"A man may have the lues and the small-pox at the same time; that is, parts of his body may be contaminated by the venereal poison, the small-pox may at the same time take place, and both diseases may appear together, but still not in the same part.

"In two eruptive diseases, when both are necessarily the consequence of fevers, and where both naturally appear after the fever nearly at the same distance of time, it would be impossible for the two to have their respective eruptions, even in different parts, because it is impossible that the two preceding fevers should be coëxistent.

"From this principle I think I may fairly put the following queries: Do not the failure of inoculation, and the power of resisting many infections, arise from the existence of some other disease at that time in the body, which is therefore incapable of another action?

"Does not the great difference in the time, from the application of the cause to the appearance of the disease, in many cases, depend upon the same principle? For instance, a person is inoculated, and the puncture does not inflame for fourteen days, cases of which I have seen. Is not this deviation from the natural progress of the disease to be attributed to another disease in the constitution at the time of inoculation? Does not the cure of some diseases depend upon the same principle?—as, e. g., the suspension or cure of a gonorrhœa by a fever.

"Let me illustrate this principle still further by one of many cases which have come under my own observation. On Thursday, the 16th of May, 1775, I inoculated a gentleman's child, and it was observed that I made pretty large punctures. On the Sunday following, viz., the 19th, he appeared to have received the infection, a small inflammation or redness appearing round each puncture and a small tumor. On the 20th and 21st, the child was feverish; but I declared that it was not the variolous fever, as the inflammation had not at all advanced since the 19th. On the 22d, a considerable eruption appeared, which was evidently the measles, and the sores on the arms appeared to go back, becoming less inflamed.

"On the 23d he was very full of the measles; but the punctures on the arms were in the same state as on the preceding day. On the 25th, the measles began to disappear. On the 26th and 27th the punctures began again to look a little red. On the 29th the inflammation increased. and there was a little matter formed. On the 30th he was seized with fever. The small-pox appeared at the regular time, went through its usual course, and terminated favorably." (Vol. iii., Treatise on the Blood, Inflammation and Gunshot Wounds—pp. 3-5.

"*All diseased actions are simple.*—A disposition of one kind may and shall exist in a part or whole, while an aciton of another kind is going on; and when the action ceases, the disposition, or dormant action, if we may be allowed to call it so, shall then come into action.   *   *   *

"Two children were inoculated for the small-pox. Their arms inflamed; but about the third or fourth day from the inoculation symptoms of fever arose, and the measles appeared, and went through their progress as usual. During this time the inflammation in the arm was arrested; but when the measles were completely gone, the small-pox took place, and went through its progress.

"Here a disposition for the measles had taken hold of the body, but although it had done that previously to the small-pox, yet it was not in such a way as stopped the progress of the small-pox. The small-pox matter was capable of contaminating, and produced inflammation, which went to a certain length, but the moment the measles changed their disposition into action, as the two actions could not go on together, the action of the small-pox was suspended till the measles had gone through its action, and the moment the constitution got free of this, the small-pox began to act again.

"A lady of rank was inoculated by Mr. Sutton. A few days after a fever came on, of the languid or putrid kind, but without any eruption, except a few petechiæ on the breast: she went through the process of a low fever, and afterwards the small-pox commenced: yet when the pustules matured they spread and were very large; also a different set of eruptions succeeded, so that thirty days passed before the skin was clear of the eruptions.

"These cases show that but one mode of action can take place at the same time; yet I could conceive that two actions might produce a third one, which might have been a new poison, as the last case in some measure seems to show." (Vol. i. Principles of Surgery—pp. 312-313.)

Dr. Joseph Adams, in his valuable Observations on Morbid Poisons, Chronic and Acute, (London, 2d Ed. 1807,) advocated the doctrine of Hunter, that "Two actions cannot be carried on at the same time, or in the same constitution." And recorded in his work the following observations to sustain this proposition.

"Though the law was entirely overlooked till Mr. Hunter's time, yet it is now as well ascertained as any other in pathology. It is worth remarking, that in all the epidemics described by Sydenham, in which small-pox and measles raged at the same season, he gives no hint of there ever appearing at the same time in the same person. Dierembroek, indeed, mentions a solitary instance in which the two diseases took place at the same time. His son remarks on the passage, that he never met with a similar instance more than twice in his own practice. Dierembroek's account is somewhat confused. It should be remarked, too, that measles was at that period not so distinctly marked as in later times, and that with the small-pox and other exanthemata, an unusual efflorescence, which may be mistaken for measles, is not uncommon. We have, however, two cases given us by that close observer, Dr. Russell, *(Medical and Chirurgical Transactions, vol. ii. p.* 90), which from the reputation of the author, deserve particular notice. The series and order of symptoms are traced with such accuracy, as not only to place the fact beyond a doubt, but to enable us to make remarks without conjectures, or with only such as every reader will see are admissable.

"We shall first observe, that when in the ill-built and crowded city of Aleppo, small-pox and measles were at the the time epidemic for three months together, only two such cases occurred. In both these cases, the measles were of a formidable kind. It is now established, that if measles do not produce their full action. they sometimes occur a second time. (See Dr. Willan's Diseases of London, p. 207.) It would be a curious enquiry, if there were any chance that it could be satisfied, to learn whether, on a future epidemic, these children took the measles again. However, those who know how few laws in pathology are without any exception, will only be surprised that this should so rarely occur.

"Dr. Settsom (Mem. of Med. Society, vol. iv., p. 288), relates the history of a family, consisting of the parents, eight children, and three servants, among whom scarlatina and measles appeared about the same time. Some had measles first, others scarlatina. All had the latter, and as many as had not gone through them before, had measles. In consequence of this succession, adds the Doctor, the diseases continued in the family for two months, which probably might have terminated in as many weeks; but no person had the two diseases at the same time, so far, at east, as could be ascertained by the symptoms !"

The industrious De Haën, wishing to discover a common original cause for all the exanthemata, remarks that small-pox and measles usually become epidemic about the same time. Referring to his notes, he observes, "that in the year 1752, scarce a family but was visited by both diseases at the same time, yet each individual had the two diseases in succession—Videas successive iisdem in aedibus occupare infantes quorum alii morbillis, variolis alii laborere demum incipiant.—*Rat. Med., vol. i., page* 102.

"Dr. Winterbottom, in a general vaccination, describes the retardation of that process, by the occurrence of measles, as an event too common to excite any particular attention. *(Med. Trans., vol. xiv., p.* 25.*)* The same retardation was remarked by Dr. King, from the same cause. *(Med. Trans., vol. xiii., p.* 167*)*. The same occurred to Mr. Wachsell, at a general inoculation in Walthamstow.

'Dr. Willan observes, that it is generally found the small-pox, measles, scarlet fever, and hooping-cough, become epidemic about the same time, and continue their progress, though not with equal violence. *(Diseases of London, p.* 105.) Yet of the three former he gives no instance in which two of them appeared at the same time in the same person. It is evident that this was not from any inadvertency, because we find the same accurate writer, on another occasion, observing that hooping cough and small-pox had occasionally occurred in the same person and at the same time. On this I would remark, that after the febrile paroxysm of hooping cough has subsided, the disease loses its specific character, and if the lungs have materially suffered, the cough may be exasperated by the variolous paroxysm. But Dr. Willan, in another place (*Diseases of London,* pp. 38–39) asserts, that in some instances hooping cough commenced during the small-pox eruption. If this fact had been furnished by a less accurate observer, I should have objected, that whenever hooping cough is epidemic, we have usually other severe coughs at the same time, which in children, are not easily distinguishable from hooping cough. But admitting the accuracy of the statement, it only proves, as Dr. Willan observes, that the law, though very general, is not without any exception. We have also his own authority, that in some instances the hooping cough was instantly superceded by small-pox, and after the decline of the latter, returned with the same violence as before. Mr. Oakes (*Medical Journal,* vol. viii., p. 426) relates the case of a child whom he was under the necessity of inoculating with small-pox whilst under the hooping Cough. The consequence was that as soon as the eruption appeared, the cough ceased, and never returned. The same has frequently happened after vaccination, and, I have reason to believe, permanently, as the cough has not returned, at least, ten days after the process of vaccination has been completed. This is now so generally understood, that many mothers have brought their children to the hospital for vaccination, under an expectation of curing them of hooping cough, and I do not recollect that any of them have been disappointed. However, I would never recommend it till the acute symptoms of the cough are passed, for, as till that time the full action of the disease is not over, it is reasonable to expect its return when the process of vaccination is completed.

"To those who are fond of tracing the operations of nature under disease, it will be curious to mark the exact regularity of the succession of these morbid poisons when they occur in the same subject. Mr. Hunter, (Introduction to Treatise on the Venereal Disease, and also to the Treatise on the Blood, &c.) found the variolous insertion in his patient interrupted on the fourth day after the puncture was made, till which time it had proceeded regularly. On the day following, the morbillous fever commenced, and on the fourth day after that, the measles appeared. Four days afterwards, the measles began to disappear. During these eight days, the variolous insertion had made no progress; but on the following day it recommenced its process, and in five days afterwards the variolous fever commenced. Here the constitutional *disposition* was interrupted on the fourth day. On its recommencement, five days more were neccessary before the *action* could take place, nine days being the medium between the insertion of small-pox and the commencement of the variolous fever.

"Mr. Cruickshanks's case (Treatise on the Absorbent Vessels, p. 126,) appears to have been interrupted *ab initio:* for he found his patient with all tne symptoms of morbillous fever on the ninth day after inoculation. The punctures of the arms, therefore, continued invisible till the constitution began to recover from the measles, after which time the punctures inflamed and required their full period of eight days for the appearance of small-pox.

"In a general vaccination at Walthamstow, two children were seized with the morbillous eruption on the eighth day after vaccination. In these the areola from that virus was suspended for four days. In a third, on the 10th day; and here the interruption to the process was only three days.

"But a most elegant experiment, in illustration of this subject, is contained in Dr. Willan's last number of Cutaneous Diseases. 'I inoculated,' says Dr. Willan, 'about the same time, three children with the fluid contained in these (lymphatic or miliary vesicles in measles), but no effect was produced by the inoculation. A similar trial, at the inoculation hospital, proved more successful. Richard Brooks, aged 18, was inoculated by Mr. Waschsel, with fluid from the miliary vesicles in the measles, and with vaccine virus, January 6, 1800. On the 10th, there was some redness and ulceration in both the inoculated places. January 15th, the redness round the part, where the lymph of the measles was inserted, had disappeared, while the vaccine pock was vivid. January 18th, the vaccine disease was over. January 22d, he has a severe cough, sneezing, and watery eyes, with cold shiverings and fainting. January 28th, the measles appeared; his eyes were inflamed and the lids swollen. January 29th, the efflorescence was diffused all over the surface of the body; frequent cough and violent fever. February 1st, efflorescence disappeared; cough and fever much abated. From that time he gradually recovered, and was dismissed in health on the 12th of February.'"

"This interesting passage, besides containing an account of the successful inoculation of the measles, affords also a striking illustration of the protraction of a disease; after the disposition of it had taken place, and its regular return to complete all its periods, as soon as the cause which interrupted them ceased. This subject was, at the same time, susceptible of the two contagions; and as long as the diseased actions were local, both went on at the same time in different parts. But as soon as the the constitutional disposition commenced in one (the vaccine), the local action from the other was suspended. When the vaccine disposition and action were completed, the rubeolous disposition commenced. Four days afterwards, the constitutional symptoms first showed themselves, with cough, sneezing, and watery eyes.* In six days more the eruptive symptoms began, and were completed on the following day. On the fourth day afterwards, the efflorescence disappeared, and the symptoms abated, making, in the whole, about twenty-seven days, a fair allowance for the two diseases.

"The following laws, then, are to be admitted with as few exceptions as any others that are received in pathology.

"1st. All persons are susceptible of the impression from a morbid poison, in proportion as they are unaccustomed to it.

"2nd. That *susceptibility* and *disposition* are necessary in a constitution or part before the action excited by a morbid poison can take place.

"3d. That after the constitutional disposition has taken place from a local diseased action, the destruction of that local action will prevent the future appearance of the constitutional disease.

"4thly. That no two actions from two different morbid poisons can be carried on at the same time in the same part, or in the same constitution.

"5thly. If a constitutional disposition to one morbid poison exists, whilst the action of another is going on in the constitution, we ought to expect the action of the first to appear after the action of the second is completed, or has ceased.

"6thly. Though nothing can prevent an *action* from following after a *disposition* has taken place, yet a *disposition* may be *prevented* by preventing a susceptibility in the constitution or part.

"7thly. The susceptibility may be prevented by rendering the constitution familiar with the morbid poison, or, as long as the constitution is exposed to it, by keeping up a constitutional action previously excited by another morbid poison, or any other cause." (*Adams on Morbid Poisons*, pp. 21-23.)

Dr. Lundford, a native of Jamaica, who made *Yaws* the subject of his inaugural dissertation states that "those who are under the *Yaws*, are liable to the other exanthemata, such as measles and small-pox. The latter may be induced by exposure or inoculation, which last is better attempted when yaws is in the decline, for then the small pox will either entirely take away yaws, or at least will check it for some time; nor will the funguses continue long, even if they should happen to appear again on the surface."

Upon this observation Mr. Adams in his work on Morbid Poisons, remarks:

"All this is perfectly analagous to what has been traced in other morbid poisons. It is probable that the irritation from small-pox and measles, being greater than from yaws, may interrupt the latter at any time. But the laws of that poison, requiring a certain course to be pursued, if the new irritation is induced before that

---

* Dr. Willan considers the common period, after infection by effluvia before these symptoms appear, to be from six to ten days. The anticipation, in this case, by inoculation, is nearly analogous to the mean difference between inoculated and casual small-pox.

course is completed, the disease must return as that new irritation ceases. If, on the contrary, that irritation has not been induced till the course of yaws is completed, and nothing remains of it but an habitual ulceration, the new irritation will not only supercede the old action, but by breaking the habit, very much expedite the cure."

" Dr. Dancer, in confirmation of the above, gives the following quotation from Dr. Membhard:—' During the universal prevalence of the small-pox in this Island, in the year 1784, it was remarked, that several negroes, afflicted with yaws, who had the yawy pustules on the surface of the body, and *had been a considerable time* under all the afflicting circumstances of the disease, were inoculated promiscuously among many other negroes. The result was that upon the decline of small-pox, and dying away of the pustules, the yaws also gradually disappeared; as if both might be considered in the light of one congenial disease." (Adams on Morbid Poisons pp. 212-213.)

Dr. Delgrade, relates several cases of the simultaneous occurrence of small-pox and measles, which ran their course together. A child was inoculated with the matter: on the eight day, this infant, after a slight indisposition, took the measles.

"On the fifteenth, having completely recovered from the measles she became very feverish. Between this and the twentieth, she had several convulsions. On that day small-pox appeared. The infant not having been near any other child with that disorder, it was thus proved not only that the eruption was variolous, but that the fever was infectious.

" Still the difficulty remained of accounting for its origin, since no small-pox was known to prevail in the neighborhood. The parents and neighbors could give no clue. Soon afterwards I heard that a child had recently died of combined small-pox and measles. Unable to trace this report, I concluded it was merely an erroneous account of the present case. Calling, however, with Mr. Daniell, on a female, one of his dispensary patients, she informed me that the child was her own. Of this case I can give no accurate narrative. The mother herself was dying, and the child had been visited by no medical attendant. Judging from the statement, I imagine the two disorders occurred in succession, not simultaneously. The child was taken ill some days before Brookes's and certainly died of small-pox. Yet even this was unsatisfactory, since the families lived at a distance from each other. No communication of the children was known, until I discovered that they had attended the same school, a circumstance of which their friends were mutually unconscious." (*Medico-Chirurgical Transactions, of London, vol. viii., Part I.*)

Dr. Russell in noticing the reciprocal influence of small-pox and measles, states that he carefully watched above 300 cases in which these diseases succeeded each other, at a time when they were both epidemic at Aleppo (1765). He noticed that the measles rarely succeeded small-pox in less than 20 days from the first appearance of the eruption. Several cases occurred where small-pox succeeded measles before the total disappearance of rubeolous rash from the extremities, that is on the 11th or 12th day of the eruption. He adds, "so little did the quality of the first disease influence that of the second, that a mild distinct small-pox was often observed to follow the worst kind of measles, and vice versâ." Wilan relates the case of a young man, aged eighteen inoculated for measles and cow-pox on the same day; the cow-pox took the lead, measles following at the end of sixteen days: and Dr. Gregory has described a case very analogous, but there measles had the start, and after sixteen days, cow-pox had its turn. Dr. Gregory calls attention to the fact, that in each case sixteen days was the period of suspension, and expresses his belief that this was not accidental. (Lectures on the Eruptive Fevers.)

Dr. Morland reported to the Boston Society for Medical Improvment the following interesting case:

On the 13th of February 1856, he vaccinated a healthy male infant, six months old. On the 17th of the same month, a faint but sufficiently distinct eruption of measles was observed about the neck and shoulders. The usual symptoms of rubeola had declared themselves on the next morning after the vaccination, and the disease, consequently, must have commenced only a few hours previously to that operation, if four days be adopted as the period elapsing between the attack and the appearance of the eruption. The vaccine vesicle matured very slowly for several days, and the rubeolous eruption continued with varying distinctness, but always comparatively slight, until the 19th, of February, when it disappeared. The vaccine vesicle then took a start, and went on rapidly to perfection. There seemed to be a retarding action reciprocally maintained for a time by the two affections, thus accidentally concurrent; vaccine finally prevailing. The circumstantial record made at the time reads thus:

"February 17th, vaccination apparently taking effect, measles appeared; will the vesicles be retarded? 18th, Vesicles advancing very slowly, measles retrograding; ordered a warm bath. 19th, Vesicles going on, but more slowly than is common;

less redness around it; eruption of measles gone; will it recur? 20th, Vaccine vesicle much larger; child feverish; warm bath. 21st, at 7¼ o'clock in the morning, the child was seized with a severe general convulsion. He was seen by Dr. M. in about twenty minutes; a warm bath had been used. Wine of ipecac, and enemata, with cold lotions to the head, were at once resorted to, and subsequently, three grains of calomel with five of rhubarb were given. Aspect of the little patient pale and confused. At 1¾ o'clock, P. M., he had another convulsive attack of rather greater severity. By previous direction, he was immediately placed in a warm bath, the body and limbs were well rubbed with the hands, and sinapisms were applied to the abdomen and to the feet; the face being colored and the scalp showing many turgid vessels, a large leech was applied to the left temple, and the wound was allowed to bleed for half an hour after the animal fell off. No more convulsions through the day. At 7½ oclock P. M., mustard was applied to the back of the neck. The night of 21st was passed by the patient in quiet sleep. 22d, very bright and well to all appearance, until 9½ o'clock, A. M., when he had another very severe convulsion, lasting several minutes longer than the two previous ones. He was seen fifteen minutes after the access of the fit; was found stupid, with an occasional wild look of the eyes; had been placed again in the warm bath. Mustard-water frictions to the extremities were continued; the head being rather hot, cold applications were cautiously made to it; one drachm of castor oil was given; discontinued the breast milk. Dr. Storer saw the patient at this time, and recommended calomel and Dovers powder, one eighth of a grain of the former to one half of a grain of the latter, every three hours. A continuance of the mustard water frictions were also advised. Dr. S. believd that another leech might be needed. Dr. James Jackson, who had been sent for at Dr. M.'s request, visited the child shortly after, and gave a favorable prognosis. It was thought best by him to restrict the child's nursing to one minute's time every two hours; and, in the intervals, to allow sugar and water. Dr. J. thought that although another leech might possibly, be required, he should 'be slow to apply it.' The remainder of the management was concurred in. The powders above mentioned were commenced, and the other means continued. There seemed a degree of amendment in the afternoon of this day, and there had been some good sleep. The night of the 22d was quietly passed: there was only one dejection; a little colicky pain from flatulence; no convulsive action. 23d, Quite well, seemingly; pulse 118, rather sharp (yesterday, 128 to 130); skin moist; one powder was taken at bedtime last evening, and another this morning. The vesicle of vaccination has broken and partially dried into quite a large scab; it was full, yesterday. In the afternoon of this day the child seemed dull and stupid, possibly from fatigue; the lips and tongue somewhat swollen; suspended the regular use of the powders; renewed the mustard frictions, etc. He was now allowed to draw the breast during three minutes, not having nursed for three hours previously. Flatulence troublesome; relieved by mint-water. 24th—Night quiet; had one dejection; got one powder about midnight; the eyes somewhat red; no signs of returning rubeolous eruption; tongue white; occasional colic. 25th—Nearly as well as ever. 26th—Same record. 27th—A cervical gland, on the left side (that of vaccination), much enlarged; otherwise very well and lively. Discontinued visits. From the last date to the present time, there has been no untoward occurrence, the child seeming better, even, than before his illness.

"The supervention of measles upon vaccination, by the doctrine of chances must be rare; a purely accidental occurrence. The points of interest in this case are the evident mutually retarding influence of the two affections thus coëxisting; the modification of the vaccine vesicle and of the eruption of rubeola by this action—not uncommonly witnessed under such, or similar, circumstances of complication—and, especially, the convulsions, as to their *cause*. Dr. M. was at first inclined to ascribe these to the retrocession of the measles; but it will be noted that they were manifested upon the eighth day after vaccination, when the vesicle should be perfect and the primary febrile action is usually observed—and consequently they may be more reasonably referred to the latter. This was Dr. Jackson's opinion. How much influence the conjunction of the two affections may have had, however, can hardly be determined. In his recently-published volume, Dr. Jackson gives an instance where convulsions took place in a child, on the eighth day after vaccination. Some time previous to this, the patient had had pneumonia, which was ushered in by convulsions, and the same had occurred, also, during dentition. Dr. J. had apprehended they might take place after the vaccination, and had forewarned the mother on the subject. He refers to other cases in which convulsions were observed in children at the commencement of bronchitis and scarlatina, but mentions only one after vaccination. In the case detailed above, there had not been any convulsions, previously, nor any threatening of them; there was, therefore, no reason to expect them.

"In this connection, the remark of Sydenham may appropriately be referred to. 'that an epileptic fit, in infants, is so sure a sign of small-pox, that if, after teething, they have one, you may predict variola—so much so, that a fit over night will be followed by the eruption next morning. This, however, will be generally mild, and in no wise confluent.' (*Works, Syd.*, Soc. edit., vol. ii., p. 252). Dr. Jackson also remarked 'that he believed convulsions are not rare in children, when the symptoms, so-called of small-pox first appear—corresponding to the eighth day of vaccination.' It would seem that the accident must be infrequent after simple vaccination." (*Boston Med. and Surg. Journ.*, June 19, 1856).

Joler has described an epidemic of measles that took place in the Retzat Circle, in Bavaria, in the district where he himself resided. He says that the disease was much milder among the vaccinated than among the unvaccinated. 15 in 52 died among the non-vaccinated, while barely 1 in 300 died among the vaccinated, showing that measels was 86 times more fatal among the former than the latter.

As far as our knowledge extends there are but few facts bearing upon the question of the possibility of the transmission of the poison of measles along with the vaccine virus.

The experiments of several authors have shown that measles may be transmitted by inoculating a sound person, either with the blood, with the fluid of the accidental vesicles which sometimes complicate the eruption, or with the secretions of those affected with the disease.

Dr. Home of Edinburgh in 1758, appears to have been the first European physician who proposed and performed the inoculation of measles. His method of inoculation was to apply cotton dipped in the blood of a measly patient to a wound in the arm of the well patient. He describes the febrile symptoms as appearing on the sixth day, and of a mild character with no secondary complications. (Clinical Facts and Experiments 1758). Mr. Wachsel, of the small-pox Hospital, in the early part of this century, inoculated successfully a lad, with fluid taken from the measly vesicles. In 1822, Dr. Speranza, an Italian physician, in the territory of Mantua, repeated the experiments of Dr. Home, Professor of Materia Medica in the University of Edinburgh. He inoculated six cases and afterwards himself, with the blood taken from a slight scratch in a vivid papula. In a few days the measles appeared; and went through their course mildly and regularly. This encouraged him to make further experiments; and he says they were all successful.

Dr. Von Katona of Borsoder, in Hungary, conducted an extensive series of experiments upon the inoculation of measles in 1842. He inoculated 1122 persons, by taking the blood and fluid from the vesicles, or a drop of the tears from a patient laboring with the disease. The operation is said to have been performed in the same manner as the inoculation for small-pox; the infecting blood was drawn from the surface most effloresced. The puncture was immediately surrounded by a red areola, which soon disappeared. On the seventh day, the fever set in with the usual premonitory symptoms of measles, as rigors and catarrhal symptoms; on the ninth or tenth day the eruption appeared; on the fourteenth desquamation commenced with decrease of fever and eruption; and on the 17th day from inoculation (7th or sometimes 8th from eruption), the patients were in general convalescent and apparently well. Dr. Katona failed only in 78 cases, out of 1112 (seven per cent.); and he affirmed that the resulting disorder was mild, contrasting favorably with the severity of the reigning epidemic. No deaths occurred among the inoculated. The fruitless and unsatisfactory experiments, which have been performed at different periods for the purpose of testing the possibility of inoculating measles, cannot be adduced as evidence against these well established facts ; far a single successful inoculation is sufficient to overthrow any number of unsuccessful attempts.

Dr. George Gregory in his valuable *Lectures on the Eruptive Fevers*, even goes so far as to express his belief that the child whose case he had detailed as having undergone cow-pox after measles, "received the germ of measles and of cow-pox at the same time ; in other words, that unknown to me the child that furnished the lymph was incubating the measles, with the zuma or poison of which the vaccine matter had become impregnated."

The following is the case as recorded by Dr. Gregory :

Eliza Finch, aged four months, residing at Pentonville, was vaccinated by me at the Small-pox Hospital, May, 15th, 1832. May 17, the child began to droop. Bilious vomiting, very severe, with drowsiness, succeeded. Much blood passed by stool. The head was very hot. Vomiting continued all that and the four following days. It ceased on the 22d. On the 24th the other febrile symptoms yielded a little. On the 25th (nine days from the invasion of symptoms, and eleven from the probable reception of the germ,) measles appeared and went through its course regularly."

Whilst the preceding facts, in the main, support the doctrine of Hunter, and show that where two poisons, representing two distinct contagious exanthematic diseases, act simultaneously upon the human being, the most obvious pathological phenomena excited by the poisons will not occur simultaneously, but in succession, the one poison retarding the action of the other, the one producing its cycle of changes, whilst the other remains dormant as it were, during the action of the other, and immediately after the changes induced by the first cease, inducing its own distinct effects: at the same time it must be admitted, that the character and course of these specific eruptive diseases, are greatly modified by such altered states of the constitution as exist in scurvy, scrofula, and secondary syphilis.

In that class of diseases represented by constitutional syphilis and scurvy, the whole mass of blood is at fault, and the nutrition is perverted, and the course and products of diseased actions are comparatively modified.

As all the nutritive processes are more or less deranged in scurvy and secondary syphilis, and as it is now established that the blood in the latter disease is capable of reproducing syphilis when inoculated in healthy bodies, and as we have shown that in scurvy the blood is so deteriorated and the forces so depressed, that the smallest injuries tend to degenerate into foul gangrenous ulcers, it is but reasonable to conclude, apart from well-established facts, that the vaccine lymph would partake of the qualities and properties of the blood from which it is formed, and the parts by which it is secreted. And even if the doctrine be maintained that the vaccine matter, as well as all other special morbid poisons, have an unvarying chemical and physical constitution, the difficulty is not removed, as in the practice of vaccination we are unable to separate the active agent of the virus, from much extraneous matter, as lymph and blood. And we contend that it is impossible to open a living vaccine vesicle and draw matter for vaccination, without injuring to a greater or less extent, the delicate blood-vessels, within and around the vesicle.

With reference to the concurrent action of the poisons of two contagious Exanthemata, upon the same system, we know nothing whatever of the state and mode of the existence of that poison which lies dormant whilst the other is acting. Does it remain in the part where it has been inserted, or does it exist as well in the blood, and affect those organs and tissues which are not implicated in the action of the first?

Until the relations and effects of each special exanthematous poison has been carefully studied, and its effects determined upon the constitution of the blood, upon the process of nutrition, upon the action of the nervous system, and upon the chemical and physical phenomena of the body, as manifested more especially in the disturbances of Circulation, Respiration and Calorification, and Excretion, it will be difficult if not impossible to settle such questions.

SECTION IV.

DRIED VACCINE LYMPH, OR SCABS, IN WHICH DECOMPOSITION HAS BEEN EXCITED BY CARRYING THE MATTER ABOUT THE PERSON FOR A LENGTH OF TIME, AND THUS SUBJECTING IT TO A WARM MOIST ATMOSPHERE.

The effects of such decomposing matter, resemble those of the putrid matter received in dissecting wounds.

The practice of some physicians to mix a considerable portion of powdered vaccine scab, with water upon a glass slide, and to use this in a number of vaccinations, from house to house, is not unattended with danger, especially during warm weather. The danger of this filthy procedure, is three-fold. First, when the dried scab is used, the chances of communicating the vaccine disease by inoculation are lessened, and there is greater danger of communicating other diseases through the medium of this dried mass of pus, blood, lymph and cellular tissue. Second, when animal matter is finely divided and mixed with water, and subjected to a temperature of near summer heat, all the conditions are supplied for those active chemical changes, which in nitrogenized matters, frequently lead to the formation of poisons, capable of exciting rapid and destructive changes in the living organism. Third, in using matter from a common store, fresh blood is frequently conveyed from the patient vaccinated, upon the instrument or lancet, to the vaccine mixture. The liability to putrefactive change is not only increased by this mixture, but also the danger of communicating secondary syphilis, or any other disease capable of being transmitted by vaccination is augmented. When a score, or more, cases are vaccinated from the same supply, and with the same instrument, if the greatest precaution is not employed, more or less blood from different individuals becomes mixed with the virus. The method so common in America, of vaccinating with the dried scab, should be entirely abandoned.

In the warm climate of the Southern States, it is especially difficult to preserve vaccine matter for any length of time, without more or less change and even putrefaction. The length of time which the vaccine virus will retain its active properties, will depend upon the temperature and the moisture of the climate.

The true mode of preserving and propagating the vaccine virus, is that recommended by Jenner, viz.: the inoculation of the lymph directly from the arm at a period not later than the eighth day. By a succession of such vaccinations upon a number of children, transported for this purpose, Dr. Francis Xavier Balmis, Surgeon-Extraordinary to the King of Spain, imparted vaccination to many nations during his voyage round the world (1803–1806) executed for the sole purpose of carrying to all the possessions of the King of Spain beyond the seas, and to those of other nations, the inestimable gift of vaccine inoculation.

At an early day in the history of vaccination, Dr. Jenner made numerous attempts to send the vaccine virus to the most distant possessions of the English in the East. After the failure of the virus sent by ships to India, he proposed that on board some ship going to India twenty recruits, or men of any description who had not had the small-pox, should be selected; and a surgeon appointed to attend the successive vaccinations. Dr. Jenner thus engaged that the vaccine disease should be carried in its most perfect state to any of the English Settlements. Upon the rejection of this proposition by the government, he formed the plan of equipping and sending out a vessel to India with such arrangements and such a number of men as to ensure the continuous transmission of the vaccine virus, by private subscirptions, and put down his own name, for one thousand guineas. Before his design could be carried into execution, tidings arrived from the east, that Dr. De Carro had succeeded in forwarding vaccine matter from Vienna to Constantinople, and from thence to Bombay. The manner in which Dr. De Carro, (by whose unwearied labors the vaccine disease was first disseminated over Germany, Venice,

Lombardy and other parts of Europe,) transmitted the vaccine virus to India, possesses great interest at the present time, when so much carelessness is manifested by the profession both in the selection and in the preservation of the virus. Many dissappointments having arisen from the difficulty of transmitting it in an active state, to distant countries, Dr. De Carro employed every expedient that ingenuity or experience could suggest to obviate them. Various methods had been tried. Impregnated lint, or threads enclosed between plates, or in bottles and in tubes closed up with wax. The practice of imbuing the points of common steel lancets was soon abandoned. To these succeeded lancets of silver, silver gilt, gold and ivory. After a series of trials, Dr. De Carro, gave the preference to ivory, which he considered to be, in all respects, the most secure vehicle for transporting the virus. On lancets of this material it was sent from Breslau to Moscow, where, under the patronage and actual inspection of the Russian Empress, it completely succeeded. As that which was destined for Bagdad would be exposed to the accidents of a long journey, in a climate heated by a scorching sun, he took special care to protect it as much as possible from external influence. He sent some on lancets of silver, silver-gilt, and ivory: he also impregnated some English lint with the vaccine fluid, and enclosed it between glasses; and when he had properly secured them he dipped them at a wax-chandler's till they formed a solid ball, which he enclosed in a box filled with shreds of paper. In this state the packet was safely conveyed across the Bosphorus, and passed over the whole line of deserts; and he had the satisfaction of hearing that, on its arrival on the banks of the Tigris, its contents were still liquid, and succeeded on the first trial. It was received on the 31st of March, 1802, upon the banks of the Tigris, and before the end of June it had reached Bombay.

Dr. De Carro, in a letter to Dr. Jenner, dated Vienna, April 22d, 1803, thus describes the method which he had employed for the preservation of the vaccine virus:

"I do not know whether you are well informed of the great improvement which M. M. Ballhorn and Stromeyer have made to the glasses invented by you. They have taught us a simple and easy manner to preserve the vaccine lymph fluid during an indefinite term. The Hanoverian Vaccinators take a small bit of English *charpie*, which you call, I believe, *dry lint*. The quantity must be, of course, equal to the concavity of the glass. The pustule then is punctured by a circular or half-circular incision with the lancet, so as to open a greater number of the cells forming the vaccine pustule covered with the same pellicle. The lint is applied upon the pustule on the most wooly side, so as to act better as a syphon. It pumps in a very short time a sufficient quantity of vaccine fluid to saturate it as completely as if it had been dipped in a glass of water, particularly if the lint is now and then gently pressed with the point or back of the lancet. When it is quite full you take it with the lancet, and place it carefully in the cavity of the glass; you put a drop of oil, or a little mucilage upon the internal surface of the glasses; you make the flat bit of glass slide upon the *charpie*, so as to exclude the air as much as possible; you tie the two bits with thread, and seal the edges. To prevent the access of light, I commonly fold it in a black paper, and when I was desired to send it to Bagdad, I took the precaution of going to a wax-chandler's, and surrounded the sealed-up glasses with so much wax as to make balls. With this careful manner, it arrived *still fluid* on the banks of the Tigris." *Life of Edward Jenner*, vol. i., pp. 420, 430.

The method so extensively employed in America, of preserving the entire scab after it seperates from the arm, by enclosing it in wax, is not only less reliable than the method practiced by Drs. Jenner and De Carro and others, but it is attended with greater danger, from the changes induced by heat and moisture.

Shortly after the introduction of vaccinatoin into the United States, by Dr. Waterhouse, ignorant persons, in New England, not of the Medical Profession, who were stimulated by avarice to carry on a traffic in vaccine matter, obtained the shirt-sleeves of patients which had been stiffened by the purulent discharge from an ulcer consequent on vaccination. These they cut into strips, and sold about the country as impregnated with the true vaccine virus. Several hundred persons are said to have been inoculated with this poison, which in some cases produced great constitutional disturbance.

SECTION V.

The Mingling of the Vaccine Virus with that of the Small-Pox; Matter taken from those who were Vaccinated while they were Laboring under the Action of the Poison of Small-Pox, was capable of producing a modified Variola, and comparatively mild Disease in

THE INOCULATED, AND WAS CAPABLE OF COMMUNICATING BY EFFLUVIA SMALL-POX IN ITS WORST CHARACTER TO THE UNPROTECTED.

In more than one instance small-pox was disseminated, by vaccination with what was considered as vaccine virus. In all such cases the virus was obtained from patients who were laboring under the action of the poison of small-pox, at the time of the insertion of the vaccine matter. Some cases of small-pox were said to have originated from the employment of small-pox scabs, which had been sent through the lines by the enemy as good genuine vaccine matter. As far as my knowledge extends, such accidents did not arise from the wilful and malicious dissemination of small-pox matter, as was charged publicly through the newspapers; but they were referable to the careless employment of vaccine matter derived from patients in small-pox hospitals, or from members of households vaccinated after small-pox had appeared in their midst, and consequently after the introduction of the poison into their systems.

Such accidents are by no means new to the profession, for more than half a century ago, they had well nigh proved fatal to the infant cause of vaccination. Many of the patients experimented upon, by Dr. Woodville at the small-pox hospital in London, were not only exposed to a variolous atmosphere, but they actually had small-pox matter inserted into their arms on the third and fifth days after vaccination. Dr. Jenner had positively asserted that pustules do not belong to the cow-pox: Dr. Woodville, on the contrary, affirmed that three-fifths of the patients whom he had inoculated with vaccine matter, had pustules not to be distinguished from variolous ones. Dr. Woodville, in an interview which he held with Dr. Jenner on the 23d of March, 1799, mentioned that the cow-pox had been communicated by effluvia, and that the patient had it in *the confluent way*. Dr. Jenner is said to have remarked on this marvellous occurrence, " Might not the disease have been the confluent small-pox communicated by Dr. Woodville, as *he* is always full of the infection ?"

Such careless experiments as those of Dr. Woodville, conducted in a *small-pox hospital!* excited the strongest feelings of disappointment among the principal medical men of London, and for a season threw doubt upon the accuracy of Dr. Jenner's statement. And it was only after careful investigation that Dr. Jenner was able to demonstrate *that the London cow-pox was somehow or other compounded with small-pox.*

This contaminated matter, from the London small-pox hospital, was distributed to different parts of the country by Dr. Pearson, and caused most unpleasant accidents. Some of this contaminated matter fell into the hands of Mr. Andrè, Surgeon at Petworth, and fourteen persons who were inoculated with it had variolus eruptions and in some cases suffered severely. Lord Egremont wrote a long letter on this occasion to Dr. Jenner, detailing the occurrence at Petworth. The reply of Dr. Jenner to this letter is worthy of careful consideration, in the light which it throws upon similar accidents occurring during the recent war.

DR. JENNER TO LORD EGREMONT.

MY LORD :—I am extremely obliged to your Lordship for your kindness in giving me so fully the account of the late inoculation at Petworth; a subject which, before, I did not clearly understand; and which, of course, had given me much vexation. I will just briefly lay before you part of the history of the cow-pox inoculation since my experiments were first publicly made known; which may tend in some measure to explain in what manner pustules may be produced.

About a twelve-month ago Dr. Woodville, Physician to the small-pox hospital, procured some virus from a cow at one of the London Milk-farms, and inoculated with it several patients at the small-pox hospital. Fearful that the infection was not advancing properly in some of their arms, he inoculated them (some on the 3d, others on the 5th day afterwards), with small-pox matter. Both inoculations took effect; and thus, *in my opinion*, a foundation was laid for much subsequent error and confusion; for the virus thus generated became the source of future inoculations, not only in the hospital, but in London, and many parts of the country.

Hearing a murmur among medical people that the cow-pox was not the simple disease I had described, but that in many instances it produced as many eruptions and was attended with as much severity as the small-pox, I went to town with the view of inquiring into tne cause of this deviation. Dr. Woodville at once invited me to the small-pox hospital, and very ingenuously told me the whole of his proceedings. The inoculated patients were shown to me, and though some were without eruptions and exhibited the appearance of the true cow-pox, others were very full of them, and I could not discern any difference between them and the perfect small-pox. I therefore did not hesitate to tell the Doctor that it clearly appeared to me that the small-pox had crept into the constitution with the cow-pox; that I did not consider them as two distinct diseases, but as *varieties* only of the same disease; and therefore they might coëxist in the same constitution, and that thus a mixed disease had been produced. I communicated also the same sentiment to Dr. Pearson, who was then, and had been, busily employed not only in inoculating from this source, but in dispensing threads embued in the virus to various places in our own country, and to many parts of the continent. Foreseeing what was likely to ensue from these hasty measures, I remonstrated against them, but was not listened to. In many places where the threads were sent a disease like a mild small-pox frequently appeared; yet, curious to relate, the matter, after it had been used six or seven months, gave up the variolous character entirely, and assumed the vaccine; the pustules declined more and more, and at length became extinct. I made some experiments myself with this matter, and saw a few pustules on my first patients; but in my subsequent inoculations there were none. From what I once saw at the hospital, I had reason to think that some of these threads sent out were not only stained with small-pox matter from the contamination spoken of, but that they had sometimes a dip in a real small-pox arm; as the patients were all mingled together at the hospital, and stood with their arms bare, ready to afford matter one among another. Without making any further trials with matter from the cow managed in another way, Dr. W. published a volume containing the result of his practice, which certainly damped the spirits of many who had from my representation taken up a high opinion of the cow-pock inoculation. A thought now struck me that, if possible, it would be proper to procure matter from a London cow, and compare its effects with that generated in the country.

Unwilling to determine in a hurry, I procured matter from a London cow, conceiving it possible that the animal in this situation might generate matter possessing qualities differing in some measure from that which is more in a state of nature in our meadows here: but the result convinced me that the virus was the same, as 500 people were inoculated from this source without the appearance of any pustules. But this history, my lord, does not tell you by what means the pustules appeared at Petworth: but it informs you how errors may arise, and how they may be persisted in. There is another source which I fear will be too common, Lancets are often carried in the pocket of a surgeon with small-pox dried upon them, for the purpose of inoculation. A gentleman some time ago sent a lancet here to have it charged, as it is called, with cow-pox matter: perceiving it stained at the point with some dried fluid, it was sent back; when he immediately recollected that his lancet was prepared with the matter of the small-pox. What confusion might have happened from this; and how narrowly we escaped it! For it was but an equal chance probably, that, had the lancet been used, a direct small-pox might have been produced; for the chances were equal whether it produced one disease or the other.

It may be necessary to observe, it is improbable that a mixture of the two matters used in this way would have produced a mixed disease, as two different diseased actions cannot go forward in one and the same part at the same time, so that the disease would have been either the perfect cow-pox or the perfect small-pox.

The matter which was made use of, I hear, came from Dr. Pearson; and doubtless Mr. Keate will have candor, and, I hope, industry enough to trace the error to its source. That there was error somewhere, of which Mr. Keate became the innocent cause, is a fact that I think will not admit of controversy. I have sometimes seen, perhaps in one case in a hundred, a few scattered pimples about the body and sometimes rashes: but these have arisen from the inflammation and irritation of the arm, for it is very well known that many acrid substances applied to the skin, so as to produce local inflammation, will frequently occasion a similar appearance."

This letter, in which Dr. Jenner announces the doctrine held and taught by his friend John Hunter, (viz., two diseased actions, cannot go forward in one and the same part, at the same time), is important not only in the demonstration which it affords of the transmission of both small-pox and cow-pox, at the same time, through the same mass of matter, but it also contains a strong argument for the view held by Jenner that these were not distinct diseases, but only *varieties* of the same disease.

Dr. Adams, in his work on Morbid Poisons, gives the following interesting and important observations, which confirm the correctness of the views of Dr. Jenner.

"It is to be hoped that a very correct attention to the processes of variolation and vaccination will enable us to ascertain the exact analogy which exists between two morbid poisons evidently distinct, yet not entirely separated by those laws which we have traced in others. The correspondence in the laws of each—the peculiarities in which they differ—the manner in which they interrupt each other's action, and the manner in which they may be made to act in concert, are all equally interesting, and are the daily subjects of experiment and observation. At present the following may be considered as established facts:

"Each, when inserted, requires about the same time to produce its local effects.

"A subject, that has regularly passed through either, is insensible to the future constitutional effects of the variolous poison.

"Each will produce secondary eruptions, having the same property of infecting as the primary; but the secondary eruptions appear more than ninety-nine times in a hundred in small-pox, and not once in three hundred, if the skin is otherwise entire in the cow-pox.

"In the small-pox, secondary pustules appear whilst the primary is advancing, and maturate two or three days after them. In cow-pox, when secondary vesicles appear, it is not till the primary has begun to scab.

"The small-pox may infect by the effluvia, the cow-pox can only be communicated by the scretion from the local infection.

"When these poisons are inserted at the same time in the same part of the same subject, by mixing the secretion of each, only one will produce its effect.

"When inserted separately in different parts of the same subject, each will produce its local effect, and at the same time.

"If cow-pox is inserted at the same time that the subject is exposed to a vitiated atmosphere, the former will supersede the effects of the latter. If inserted four days later, the effect will be less certain, but as far as can be ascertained, not more uncertain than from the variolous insertion." (Adams on Morbid Poisons, p. 10–16.) Dr. Adams gives several instances to show that the vaccine and variolous diseases may be confounded in certain cases, that is, that the laws peculiar to one may occasionally influence the other. (See pp. 16–20.)

"The invaluable Jennerian discovery has introduced us to a morbid poison, the properties of which are different from all others that we are acquainted with in superseding the constitutional susceptibility to another. As such a law as this is unknown in any other two morbid poisons, we might suspect the analogy between these two would be clearer than between any other two. We might even expect that the characters of the two might be altered by applying both at the same time, and also that the phenomena of one might imitate the phenomena of the other in such a manner, as to render the distinction between the two often doubtful. It is therefore, rather a matter of surprise that the distinction should be so regularly preserved, and the laws which separate other morbid poisons so rarely infringed.

"The next thing I would remark, is that small-pox and cow-pox, contrary to the law of all morbid poisons, which are different in their action, will proceed together in the same person, without the smallest interruption of each other's course. If inserted nearly at the same time, in the same person, each proceeds in the same course as if it were in two different subjects: if inserted nearly in the same spot, the two form one common areola, but the vesications are distinct, and each preserves its own character, till that of small-pox becomes purulent from suppuration for the the separation of the slough. If secondary pustules follow from the small-pox, and they should continue coming ont till the cow-pox has completed its progress, its vesicle, like any other inflamed part, will become the seat of a small-pox pustule, or the whole vesicle will become purulent, contrary to its legitimate character. In the first case, you may take small-pox matter from the pustule, which, by the adhesive inflammation, will remain distinct from, though seated in part of the vaccine vesicle; and from the other parts of the vesicle you may take the vaccine matter, and each will perpetuate its respective morbid poison. If the whole vesicle becomes purulent, it is a variolous pustule, and will inoculate small-pox.

"It was remarked by Dr. Woodville, that if a person is inoculated with small-pox to-day, and three or four days after is reïnoculated with the same morbid poison, though the last insertion may remain a smaller pustule than the first, yet both inoculations will arrive at their height at the same time. The same takes place in cow-pox; and also, if a person is inoculated to-day with cow-pox, and three or four days after with small-pox, or to-day with small-pox, and three or four days after with cow-pox, the two insertions, though the last may remain smaller than the first, will maturate and scab at the same time.

"By these facts it appears, first, that a marked kind of small-pox may be perpetuated. If, therefore, the cow-pox is a marked kind of small-pox, there can be no reason why it should not have been perpetuated with its true character; and that the cow-pox is such, appears, secondly, by its not being interrupted by, and not interrupting the progress of small-pox, and by both retaining their respective laws and characters at the same time, whether inoculated separately in different subjects, or the same; or if each has been inoculated in the same subject at different times, the consequence is similar to the inoculation of either one, at different times.

"These experiments have been repeated so often, as to leave no question concerning the law. The same experiments have been repeatedly tried with small-pox and measles, and also with cow-pox and each of the others, yet these interruptions have always followed, which have been remarked in the early part of the work.

"As therefore, a marked variety of small-pox is capable of preserving its distinct character under inoculation, there seems no reason why the cow-pox should not be among such varieties; and as any of the known varieties will destroy the susceptibility to the disease in all other forms, so there is no reason why cow-pox, if among the varieties, should not do the same; and there is the more reason to expect this, because, contrary to any other morbid poisons, the action of small-pox and cow-pox are maintained at the same time in different parts of the same constitution, subject respectively to similar laws, whether only one or both of them are applied in any variety of forms.

"It may be said that small-pox is an eruptive disease, whilst cow-pox, though affecting the constitution, is only confined in its local action to a single part. But small-pox is sometimes, we have seen, equally confined in its local action, and principally in those cases in which its appearance most resembles cow-pox. It is not less certain that cow-pox, on some occasions, produces secondary eruptions. Besides the cases I have seen myself, the Rev. Mr. Holt (Med. and Phys. Journal) gives an account of full eruption of vesicles, which had the same properties of contagion as the inoculated part. The Rev. Mr. Fernn saw a few scattered in different parts." (Adams on Morbid poisons, pp. 398-401.)

Dr. Willan found "that when a person was inoculated with vaccine and variolous matter about the same time, (that is, not exceeding a week,) both inoculations proved effective, for the vaccine vesicle proceeded to its acme in its usual number of days, and the maturation of the variolous pustule was attended by a variolous eruption on the skin." (On Vaccine Inoculation, p. 1.)

When cow-pox is inserted during the incubative stage of the casual small-pox, while the small-pox is still latent, the vaccine vesicle for the most part does not advance, or advances tardily and imperfectly. There are exceptions, however, to this rule, and cow-pox and casual small-pox may sometimes be seen running their full course at the same time. In no case, however, does the cow-pox so inserted alter or modify the course of the small-pox. When the variolous and vaccine fluids are inserted into the arms on the same day, each disease occasionally proceeds, preserving its original character. At other times, however, they mutually restrain and modify each other. The vaccine vesicle is smaller than usual, and irregular in its progress, while the variolous pustules which follow are of the kind denominated *variolæ verrucosae*, vulgarly swine-pock, stone-pock, or horn-pock (*Willan on Vaccine Inoculation*, p. 5); that is to say they are hard and shining, surrounded with little inflammation, and they suppurate imperfectly. The small quantity of matter they contain is absorbed, leaving the cuticle horny and elevated for many days afterwards. Upon the extremities the eruption does not pustulate at all, but is minute and papulous, and terminates by desquamation. It will be found in most cases that even though the eruption be modified in its character, there is nevertheless considerable disturbance of the general system under the joint influence of the variolous and vaccine poisons.

Dr. Woodville has said that if the cow-pox matter and the small-pox matter be both inserted in the same arm of a patient, even within an inch of each other, so that on the ninth day the same efflorescence becomes common to both the local affections, nevertheless inoculating from the cow-pox tumor the genuine vaccine disease will be produced (*Observations on the Cow-pox*, p. 12); but if the inoculation be performed with a mixture of the two matters, then the chance is equal that small-pox or cow-pox will be the result, or the varioloid disease.

When the insertion of the vaccine lymph *precedes* that of the variolous by a period not exceeding four days, both diseases advance locally. Sometimes an eruption of small-pox papulæ follows. At other times the variolus fever is slight and unaccompanied by eruption. Under these circumstances, matter taken from the primary vesicles shall sometimes communicate cow-pox and small-pox respectively, but more commonly the variolous poison predominates, and contaminates the lymph of the vaccine vesicle. It was ignorance of this phenomenon, in the mutual action of the vaccine and variolous poisons, which occasioned Dr. Woodville's mistakes at the small-pox hospital in 1799.

Variolous matter inserted into the arm at any period not exceeding a week from the date of vaccination will take effect and be followed by a pustule. After that time no effect is produced.

When small-pox inoculation precedes by three or four days the insertion of vaccine lymph, the vaccination advances, but after the tenth day the fluid in the vaccine vesicle becomes purulent; and in that state will communicate small-pox. (Willan on Vaccine Inoculation, p. 8 ; also Dr. George Gregorie's valuable article on Vaccination in the Cyclopædia of Practical Medicine.)

Dr. Denby, whilst admitting that the period of incubation of variola may be somewhat undefined, as in the case of other animal poisons, concludes that nevertheless, from experiments, a fair conclusion may be formed as to the usual period of this incubation, when vaccine prophylaxis may be induced. And from these Dr. Denby judged that, if on the third day, before the onset of erethism, rigor, and headache, perfect lymph be inserted, prophylaxis is almost certain, assuming three or four days for the premonitory symptoms before the variolous point or papula appears. The vaccine vesicle will then be eight or nine days old, the areola will be becoming indurated, and erethism will exist. Dr. Denby considers that in this fever against fever, the essence of prophylaxis really exists. If under this influence the variolous papula proceeds, it will resemble umbilicated varicella or horn-pock. If the vaccine be used two days later, especially if there be bronchial or pulmonary symptoms present, it will be useless. The papula may be just apparent, but it will be blighted. There are of course exceptions to this rule. A woman was delivered, says Dr. Hennen, while suffering from confluent variola ; the infant was vaccinated a few hours after birth. The mother died on the 11th day ; the infant had true vaccine, and lived. (Med. Times, Oct. 25, 1851). In an analagous case reported by Mr. T. C. Beatty of Durham, the child delivered from a mother in whom the variolous pustules made their appearance during labor, was not vaccinated until the morning of the fourth day after its birth. True vaccine was the result ; and yet, on the eigth day after she was vaccinated, when the vesicles were fully matured, the little patient was very ill, and showed signs of an eruption under the skin, which proved to be *confluent* small-pox, of which the little creature died four days after. (London Lancet, 1852.)

Dr. Robert Fowler of the Loughborough Dispensary, and Mr. Robert Tod of Gilmore Place, Edinburgh, (London Lancet, 1852); M. M. Herard and Bousquet, (L'Union Médicale, Nos.

108, 109, 110, Bulletin de Thérapeutique, tom. xxxv., pp. 342–52), and others, have recorded cases proving the possibility of the simultaneous existence of small-pox and the vaccine disease, and confirming the correctness of the conclusions of Jenner and the older observers.

M. Bousquet goes so far as to deny that the two eruptions, variola and vaccinia, exert any reciprocal reaction, and the nearer they appear together, the more independent are they of each other. Suppose, for example, that they could appear at the same hour, then each would pursue its ordinary course, just as if the other were not present. But supposing the one eruption appears after the other, all will depend upon the space of time separating them. If this be only some hours, or even two or three days, all passes on as just stated. The case is different when one of these eruptions is greatly in advance of the other. If this is not to such an extent as to exclude, the eruptions progress together, but not in parallel. The most advanced always keeps its advantage, and finishes at its ordinary epoch, without having undergone any change in form or duration. The other follows it at a distance, but after the variolous capacity of the subject has become exhausted by the first, the second dies away. In these influences, M. Bousquet considers that there is nothing direct, active or special, they are the consequences of the faculty possessed by the eruptions of supplying or substituting each other. The vaccinia does not arrest the variola, but it is the variola that stops short in the face of the vaccinia; and, conversely, variola does not 'cut short the course of vaccinia, but this last interrupts its own course in presence of the variola. It is the right of precedence, and the more widely the two eruptions are separated, the more readily do they exclude each other, while the nearer they are together, the more independently do they proceed. Considered in themselves, the vaccine and variolous virus are so little capable of destroying each other's energy, that if they are mixed together, and inoculation performed with the mixture, M. Bousquet affirms that two perfectly distinct eruptions may be produced. Considered as regards their effects, therefore, according to this view, it cannot be said that vaccinia *cures* variola, or even, rigorously speaking, that it *prevents* it. It takes its place, stands in its stead, and is neither more nor less than a substitution. Thus, so far from explaining the operation of vaccinia by the supposed opposition it offers to variola, we would rather do so by the analogy and reciprocal action of the two diseases. (Bulletin de Thérapeutique, tom. xxxv., pp. 342–52 ; also The British and Foreign Medico-Chirurgical Review, April, 1849.)

From the facts recorded in this section, we deduce the practical conclusions :

First—That vaccine matter derived from the patients of small-pox hospitals, or from those in civil or military practice who have been exposed to the contagion of small-pox, should never be used for the propagation of the vaccine disease.

Second—The vaccine disease is not a distinct disease from small-pox, but a variety or modified form of the variolous affection.

SECTION VI.

DRIED VACCINE LYMPH OR SCABS, FROM PATIENTS WHO HAD SUFFERED WITH ERYSIPELAS DURING THE PROGRESS OF THE VACCINE DISEASE, OR WHOSE SYSTEMS WERE IN A DEPRESSED STATE FROM IMPROPER DIET, BAD VENTILATION, AND THE EXHALATIONS FROM TYPHOID FEVER, ERYSIPELAS, HOSPITAL GANGRENE, PYÆMIA, AND OFFENSIVE SUPPURATING WOUNDS.

In several instances during the revolution death resulted from PHLEGMONOUS ERYSIPELAS, following vaccination in apparently healthy patients, in both civil and military practice.

It was believed that in some cases the poison of ERYSIPELAS was conveyed along with the vaccine virus.

In one instance which came to my knowledge, the lives of several negro women and children were destroyed by Erysipelas excited by vaccine matter taken from the same scab, and a stout healthy white man who was vaccinated with the same matter, and by the same physician who vaccinated the negroes (on a neighboring plantation,) was extremely ill from the effects of the poisonous matter, and barely escaped with the loss of a large portion of the muscles of the arm.

I was informed upon good authority that this matter caused the death of a pregnant negro woman, and of another negress and her young infant, of some week or ten days of age, at the time of the inoculation of the vaccine virus.

The following observations relating to Erysipelas following vaccination, were placed in my hands, by Dr. Frank A. Ramsay, of Memphis, Tennessee:

Communicability of Syphilis by Vaccination. By WM. GERDNER. M. D., of Green County, Tennessee.

I notice in the "Medical and Surgical Monthly—June, 1866," an article taken from the Richmond Medical Journal, June, 1866, by Wm. Fuqua, M. D. Appomatox county, Virginia, on the Communicability of Syphilis by Vaccination.

About the same time referred to by Dr. Fuqua, I had numerous cases of vaccination, in the district of my practice, presenting abnormal features. The people believed it to result from Syphilis, and called the exhibitions by that name. I made close scrutiny of the cases, occurring under my observation, and concluded that they were not syphilitic in origin or manifestation. I regarded them as Erysipelas, presenting the form called Phlegmonous: for which opinion I thought I had reasons. Many cases assumed the form of common Erysipelas, invading limited portions of the arm; and in some few cases the whole surface of the vaccinated limb was affected.

The proper distinction for the practical physician of Erysipelas, is Superficial and Deep Seated—ordinary or common Erysipelas affecting the cuticle proper— deep seated or phlegmonous Erysipelas involving the tissues, particularly the cellular. At present the cause of the difference is inexplicable—why in one case serum, and in the other lymph is poured out, remains a question, while the fact exists. Each distinct inflammation has its habits."

As far as my knowledge extends, the records of medicine do not afford any very large collection of cases of Erysipelas supervening upon vaccination. The following are the most important cases of the apparent excitation of Erysipelas by vaccination, which were noted in the works and journals consulted during these researches:

Diffuse Cellular Inflammation following Vaccination.—The first was that of a female child, aged five years, who had been vaccinated by a respectable practitioner in Dublin. This child was brought to the physician who reports these cases, about three weeks after it had been inoculated. The arm was then greatly swollen, the swelling extending to the hand; the integuments of the upper arm were of a dusky leaden hue, and a large black slough occupied the situation of the usual crust of the vaccine vesicle. The child's pulse was weak and slow, not exceeding 64. The extremities were cold, tongue dry and coated. There were extensive sloughing and hemorrhage from the mucus membrane of the mouth. The integuments of the cheeks adjoining the commissure of the lips were of a livid hue. The respiration was very much hurried, but no physical sign of disease could be detected in the chest.

The child's parents stated that these formidable symptoms first presented themselves, between the ninth and twelfth day from that on which it had been vaccinated. The practitioner who inoculated the child affirmed that up to that period, the vaccine vesicle ran a healthy course, and that he had vaccinated other children with the same lymph in whom the course of the vesicle was perfectly regular. This child was of a delicate constitution, having sufferd with attacks of scrofulous ophthalmia, pneumonia, and bronchitis. Its health was said to be good, at the time it was inoculated. Complete recovery, though very slow, was effected in this case by the use of mild tonics and stimulants.

The second case was that of a male child, aged eighteen months, who was also vaccinated by a physician of Dublin. About the twelfth day from the period on which it was vaccinated, the arm was attacked with severe inflammation of the erysipelatous character, the vaccine vesicle having, up to that day, according to the statements of the parents, run a regular course. On the sixteenth day, a dark slough, as large as a shilling, occupied the situation of the vesicle; the entire extremity was immensely swollen; the integuments of the upper arm were of erysipelatous redness, and such of them as were in the immediate neighborhood of the slough were quite livid. The attending fever was of the inflammatory type, the skin being hot, tongue furred, pulse rapid and full, and the thirst great. Until the fever was subdued by cooling and alterative medicines, and the local inflammation relieved by the application of poultices and fomentations, the sloughing spread with the most alarming rapidity. After the sloughs had separated, and the progress of the gangrene arrested, a large and deep ulcer remained with undermined edges, at the bottom of which the muscles of the arm could be distinctly observed; so extensive was this ulcer, that it was not healed for three months, though the case progressed most favorably in every respect."—*Dublin Journal of Medical Sciences*, 1844.

Dr. Greene reported to the Boston Society for Medical Improvement, a fatal case of erysipelas, following re-vaccination, which occurred in January. 1846.

The patient, a gentleman sixty-four years of age, had been vaccinated twenty years before, and re-vaccinated, though without success, two or three times since. On Friday, the day after the re-vaccination by Dr. Greene, he was seized with chills, nausea, and a sense of general uneasiness; and, at the same time, inflammation commenced in the arm, attended with heat, redness, and pain. He slept none on the following night, and on the next night was attacked with vomiting and purging. The symptoms from this time did not become materially worse, however, till the following Wednesday, when he complained of pain just below the elbow; and on Thursday, a small patch of erysipelas was discovered at this point, which gradually extended over the arm and chest of the affected side, the infiltration of the cellular tissue, keeping about two inches ahead of the redness. He died at ten on Friday evening, a little more than eight days from the time of re-vaccination, the erysipelas having extended to within two inches of the sternum. In regard to the quality of the matter introduced, Dr. Greene remarked that it was taken on the eighth day from a perfectly formed vesicle, on the arm of a perfectly healthy infant, born of healthy parents; that one of his own children had been vaccinated with the same matter, and also another person, in both which cases, the symptoms and appearances were slight.

It is said that in 1849 and 1850, Erysipelas so frequently followed vaccination in Boston, and the result was so often fatal, that many physicians refused to vaccinate, except when it was absolutely necessary, and almost entirely abandoned re-vaccination. Cases were reported to the Boston Society for Medical Improvement, by Drs. J. B. S. Jackson, Cabot, Bigelow, Homans, Putnam, and Channing. From the transactions of this society we select the following cases:

Case Reported by Dr. Cabot.—This being a case rather of diffuse cellular inflammation than common erysipelas. The patient was a gentleman, sixty-nine years of age, who having been exposed to varioloid, was re-vaccinated in two places on the 3d of April. On the second day, two vesicles had formed about the size of a small pin's head, and there was pain in the axilla, with pain and soreness under the pectoral muscles. In about two weeks the inflammation had extended to the hand, and in the course of the third week an opening was made about the elbow, from which a considerable quantity of sero-purulent fluid was discharged; the back of the hand being opened down to the fascia a few days afterwards. From the shoulder the erysipelas extended over the whole back, down the right arm to the elbow, and somewhat over the abdomen from each side; also across the front of the chest, nearly to the right shoulder. The whole duration of the erysipelas in an active form was about seven or eight weeks; neither the hand nor lower extremities were affected; the areola about the vaccine points subsided, but subsequently this surface was attacked with the disease. The suppuration about the left shoulder and down the upper extremity, had been very extensive; the pectoral muscle was separated from the parietes of the chest, and the skin of the forearm was so detached from the subjacent parts that fluids thrown in at the elbow would pass out at the back of the hand; very numerous openings have been made about the elbow and shoulder for the discharge of pus. For about two months the patient was confined to his bed, and convalescence was tedious. The prostration was not so great as would have been expected in such a case; the pulse not rising above ninety during the active stage of the inflammation; there was, however, some delirium, with chills, headache and pain in the back. No suppuration occurred, except in the parts above alluded to.

Case Reported by Dr. J. Bigelow.—This patient was a gentleman, about thirty years of age, and having been exposed to the small pox, was re-vaccinated with several others, from the same virus. Two days afterwards, an erysipelatous spot, of the size of a dollar, was discovered around the point of vaccination. This spread rapidly in every direction, and at the end of five days, had occupied the whole arm from the shoulder to the elbow. At this time, several dark spots appeared upon the inside of the arm, which in two days were perfectly gangrenous, so that an incision was made five inches in length, without pain. The slough was apparantly confined to the skin and cellular substance, inasmuch as the muscular power was at no time lost. Meanwhile the pulse was quick, and the skin hot, with prostration, headache and delirium. In another week, the erysipelas had extended to the whole trunk, half way down the thighs, and to the wrist of the affected arm; the patient being much of the time delirious, or somnolent, and with a pulse of 120. During the third week, the symptoms were greatly aggravated, and the cerebral affection increased; there was also a retention of urine, and the catheter was required for a fortnight. During this time, however, the slough gradually separated, leaving a large, deep ulcer. The patient became convalescent at the end of a month, and slowly recovered; the ulcer requiring another month or more to cicatrize. No other person, who was vaccinated with the same virus, had any unusual symptoms; but a lady of the family, about seven weeks after the vaccination, was attacked with inflammation of the fauces and tonsils, followed by prostration and delirium, and died in a week; during her sickness a livid spot, about two inches in diameter, appeared over the upper part of the sternum, but this disappeared before death.

In another case reported by Dr. Bigelow; a healthy child about five months old, was vaccinated, and the vesicle went on well until the ninth day, when the arm became erysipelatous, the inflammation rapidly spreading over the whole trunk; and the child died in a few days. On the eighth day of the vesicle, the day before the appearance of the erysipelas, matter was taken with which three others were vaccinated, and these patients had perfect vesicles without any anomalous symptoms.

Case Reported by Dr. Homans.—The patient was a healthy infant, about three weeks old. On the eighth day, the vesicle appeared well, and matter was taken with which other children were vaccinated, the result being in every case successful. On the tenth day, erysipelas appeared below the elbow, and extended into the axilla; the swelling and redness were very defined, and the inflammation spread rather more rapidly than is usual in the adult. Vomiting and diarrhœa came on, and lasted for some days; and the pulse was too quick to be counted. The head and abdomen then became affected, and on the ninth day from the invasion of the disease, the scrotum and penis were greatly swollen; these last were punctured with much relief, but a deep sloughing of the scrotum took place, one and a half inches in diameter, and nearly exposing the testicles. The extremites were next affected, but in the mean time the child began to improve, and the pulse had fallen to 120 On the subsidance of the disease, abcesses formed upon the body and limbs beneath the surface, and about the left hip, one that was quite large and deep. This last, is the only one that remains open, and the child is fairly convalescent, after a sickness of about three months.

Dr. Channing mentioned a case of Erysipelas, after vaccination, in which the shoulder, axilla, and pectoral muscles were involved.—(The American Journal of the Medical Sciences, Oct., 1850—pp. 318–321.)

Dr. Charles E. Buckingham, Physician to the Boston House of Industry, has also published an interesting case of "Constitutional Irritation following Vaccination," from which we make the following abstract:

B——, a farmer, twenty-five years of age, of previous robust health, vaccinated on Thursday, August 28th, 1849.

Sept. 1st, he took an emetic, and on the 2d a cathartic dose. Both operated freely. Dr. Buckingham was first called to him at 9, P. M., September 3d. At this time the patient presented the following condition:—Complete anorexia; great thirst; headache; sleeplessness; pain in back; eyes and hearing normal; urine free; pulse 120, full and strong; decubitus dorsal. His late vaccination was not known at this time. Got a saline mixture, consisting principally of bicarbonate of soda and chlorate of potassa.

4th. Febrile action less; has pain in calf of right leg; no tenderness, redness, swelling, or heat.

9th. Pulse 84; appetite good. No sleep last night on account of the pain in the calf, and in the sole of the right foot; has had a sinapism to the foot, with partial relief; no dejections for twenty-four hours; whole of right calf swollen; a circumscribed red spot one and a half inches below head of right fibula, covering about two square inches.

10th. Patient was seen, in consultation, by Dr. H. G. Clark. Redness more diffused; leg much swollen, and œdematous from knee to heel; pain confined to the spot of yesterday, which is, for the first time, tender; no headache or thirst; eyes and hearing normal; neither delirium nor sighing; no appetite; tongue red at its top, and in other parts covered with a thick creamy paste; pharynx the same; pulse 88, full.

13th, 9, A. M. Pulse 100, full and soft; no dejection. Attention was called to a hard, red, circumscribed swelling on the left forearm, similar to the others; in examining which, found the remains of an irregular vaccination, of which Dr. Buckingham first learned the date as given above.

16th. Swelling of right leg decidedly less; that of the left leg hard, red, and excessively tender. The right elbow was red and swollen. The right eye red, swollen, and painful about the orbit; no conjunctival redness; tears trickling over face; pulse 120, full, soft, dicrotic; respiration slow and distinct, with occasional sighing; no delirium; tongue perfectly steady, when protruded; face somewhat livid; no dejection for two days, except from enemata.

18th. Had a good night; pulse 112; respiration 16; nose much swollen, dusky, red, and painful; about a dozen papules, hard, red, and shot-like, scattered over forehead, face, back, and legs; no glandular enlargement. 12 M., a few more papules on abdomen; the others are becoming pustular, and a few are umbilicated.

19th, 8½ A. M. Two dejections, with urine; tongue dry, black, and cracked; redness and swelling of whole upper face; papules increasing in number, and pustules in size; a few of them umbilicated; no glandular enlargement.

20th, 10 A. M. Pulse 120, more firm, but not so full; respiration 32, laboured, no rales; numerous black, pasty dejections; took oss of brandy in the night; restless, and occasionally wandering; easily roused, and speaks sensibly, but soon falls asleep again; pustules increasing in size and number, some of them as large as good-sized peas; knuckles of right hand swollen; both sides of face red, swollen, and œdematous; right leg of normal size, and appears well; left leg the same, with the exception of slight tenderness; swelling of left forearm soft and fluctuating; no glandular enlargement, nor mark of absorbents.

9 P. M. Constantly delirious; unable to drink; frequent involuntary dejections and urine; hands tremble, pulse 134, feeble; respiration 36, noisy and husky; sounds and impulse of heart normal; many of the pustules drying; scab of vaccination came off arm; erythema and œdema of scalp.

21st, 10 A. M. Delirious all night; takes nothing; insensible; no dejections; pulse 134, soft, and moderately full; respiration varies from 30 to 40, occasionally like that in hydrophobic paroxysm; heart's impulse strong; first sound loud, second sound scarcely perceptible.

5¼, P. M. Died. The body was removed early next day. No autopsy allowed."

As far as Dr. Buckingham could learn, there had been no sick animal on his farm, and so far as known, the patient had had no communication with any such, nor had he any occasion to handle hides.—*The American Journal of the Medical Sciences*, July, 1850—pp. 96-99.

Doctor Paul F. Eve does not admit the possibility of the inoculation of erysipelas by vaccination, as will be seen from the following extract from his article on the health of the Southern Army:

"Erysipelas by Vaccination. In regard to the innoculation of erysipelas by vaccination, independent of a peculiar atmospheric influence, and irrespective of some adventitious circumstance connected with a wound, I am not prepared to admit. We are all familiar with the idiopathic variety of this affection attacking the cutaneous and mucous surfaces, at times, too, becoming epidemic, and apparently in affinity with puerperal peritonitis, and we know the traumatic type; but surely this disease does not originate from a specific virus. It is evidently infectious, but not, I believe, contagious. A distinguished surgical writer, admitting that it is inoculable, states expressly that it would be impossible for it ever to appear in a sound individual.

There, then, must be a predisposition in the general system, it would seem in every nstance, usually induced by malaria, before it is developed. And if this be true, namely, that the attack depends for its origin upon a peculiar state and condition of the patient's health, is it not then unwise, not to say erroneous, to suppose that erysipelas occuring after vaccination is due to a poison escorted by vaccine matter into the system? I do not, therefore, believe it inoculable by this little operation."

The view maintained by Hippocrates and his followers, that Erysipelas was a disease originating from some intestine commotion of the humors, and that the offending matter was thrown off or eliminated by means of the skin, has been held by a large number of writers, with various modifications and slight additions up to the present time. The French writers especially advocate this view, and as a general rule deny the contagiousness of Erysipelas. The English writers, on the other hand, are almost unanimous in considering the disease as capable of propagating itself by contagion under certain circumstances. Dr. Cullen admitted a species of Erysipelas capable of throwing off contagious emenations. He says, " This disease is not commonly contagious, but as it may arise from an acrid matter externally applied, so it is possible that the disease may sometimes be communicated from one person to another."

The first well-authenticated facts militating against the old notions, and proving the contagious nature of Erysipelas, were published by Dr. Wells in 1798 : for although Sauvages, in his " Nosologia Methodica," published thirty years before, admits an *Erysipelas contagiosum*, his views are obscure and his authority doubtful, as the epidemic of Tolouse in 1715, to which he refers in support of his opinion, appears to have been Scarlatina, and not Erysipelas. The examples brought together by Dr. Wells, in which this complaint appeared to be unequivocally propagated by contagion, have been sustained by similar cases, described by Pitcairn, Stevenson, Gibson, Lawrence, Gregory, Elliotson, Arnott, Watson, Rogers, Goodfellow, and other English Physicians.

The question of the possibility of communicating the poison of Erysipelas along with the virus of the vaccine disease, is intimately associated with that of the contagiousness of Erysipelas.

There was a diversity of opinion amongst the Confederate

surgeons with regard to the contagiousness of Erysipelas. This diversity of opinion was clearly referable in some cases to dogmas embraced during education, and to a want of careful and extended observation, and investigation of the origin, and mode of propagation, of the diseases incident to camp life. The reliability and value of the testimony of men upon such questions, clearly depends, not merely upon the extent of the field of observation, but also upon the mode in which, and the intelligence with which, the phenomena are investigated.

Many cases occurred during the progress of the war, in which Erysipelas was clearly referable in its origin and spread to the crowding together of large numbers of sick and wounded, in ill-ventilated hospitals.

The following communication from Dr. J. C. Nott, of Mobile, Alabama, illustrates, not only the dependence of Erysipelas upon crowding, but also shows that in such cases, in like manner with Hospital Gangrene, the disease is best eradicated by scattering the patients and giving them free ventilation. It would be surely unwise and unphilosophic to refer the origin of Erysipelas in such cases to an atmospherical influence, for the disease was most prevalent and most fatal in the most crowded hospitals, and was most speedily and effectually destroyed by breaking up those sources of contagion.

No light whatever is thrown upon the subject, by declaring the disease *infectious* and not contagious in crowded hospitals. We can only refer the propagation of infectious diseases to the exhalations from the sick, or from the excretions of their bodies, which act upon the extended surface of the lungs and skin of those immersed in the infected atmosphere: and we know that in the case of the two most *contagious* and *infectious* diseases, Small-pox and Measles, the diseased actions may be propagated in both ways by the inhalation of the exhalations of the sick, as well as by direct contact with the morbific matters.

MOBILE, 21st Nov., 1866.

DEAR SIR: Your letter came to hand yesterday, together with two Nos. of your Journal. I am sorry that I have no notes or statistics relating to Hospital Gangrene. My connection with the army was in the Command of Gen. Bragg, commencing about six weeks before the battle of Shiloh. I had, it is true, been the Medical Director in Mobile for some time previously, but we had no wounds to deal with. Very soon after we got to Corinth, all sorts of camp diseases prevailed among the troops—diarrhœa, typhoid fever, &c., and erysipelas. The Colonel of a regiment came to me and begged me to visit a small brick church in the suburbs of Corinth, in which his men were dying at a fearful rate with Erysipelas. On visiting the church, I found some seventy or eighty sick and wounded men crowded together in a small church, and about one half of them with Erysipelas. There had been daily skirmishing going on, and about one fourth of the men had been wounded, The disease attacked those wounded, as well as others, indiscriminately. Many of them were dying of Erysipelas of face and scalp, who had not been wounded, and I never saw a more revolting scene than this hospital presented. ' I ordered it to be evacuated at once, and the patients to be removed to tents, at some distance off in the open field. The effect was immediate and salutary. The Erysipelas ceased to attack others, and the health of the command improved rapidly.

At the same time above alluded to, we had some cases of Hospital Gangrene among the wounded in different hospitals, up to the time of the battle of Shiloh. Being occupied very busily in office as Director of the Post, I had no time for visiting hospitals, and the battle of Shiloh coming off soon, and there being very little hospital accommodation, we were compelled to send off in every direction 10,000 wounded and as many sick. So I saw very little of what occurred among our wounded.

I afterwards went into Kentucky; was at the battle of Perryville, and other smaller battles; but here we had to leave our wounded behind, after every battle.

So really my experience has not been extensive or satisfactory in Hospital Gangrene. I have seen a good many scattering cases during the war, and have found them best treated by the application of Nitric Acid, Iron, tonics, stimulants, and good diet.

On the whole, then my observations and information are too indefinite to be worth much, and I write more to state the simple fact that we did have cases of Hospital Gangrene before and after the battle of Shiloh, and I looked upon it as close akin to Erysipelas.

Very Respectfully, Yours, &c., J. C. NOTT.
Prof. JOSEPH JONES, Nashville.

It will be seen from the following statistical information and sanitary report of the Moore Hospital, Manassas Junction, Virginia, for the month of January, 1862, that in this hospital, which received the worst cases of Typhoid Fever and Pneumonia, and which was liable to sudden and unavoidable crowding of the sick, Erysipelas attacked almost universally the patients operated on, only two escaping.

"MOORE HOSPITAL," MANASSAS JUNCTION, VA., February 7, 1862.
THOS. H. WILLIAMS, Surgeon C. S. A., Medical Director Army of Potomac:
SIR: I have the honor to forward the report of the "Sick and Wounded" of the

Moore Hospital, for the month of January. The face of it shows only 235 patients admitted, while 77 of these have died—a fearful mortality, I confess—and did it extend to all diseases treated, would soon decimate our army. But when it is recollected that the 235 men kept here were picked out of over 2,900 that have passed through and were sent further back, and that those kept are the sickest—in fact a number came in moribund, others dying from six to twenty-four hours after their arrival—the mortality does not appear so appalling. At the beginning of January, here were remaining 114 sick and convalescents; of these 25 died during the past month, making the mortality 102. The report shows 37 cases of febris typhoides, with 17 deaths, which is, strictly speaking, not true, as there have been but 4 or 5 cases of well-developed typhoid fever in the wards, and those so diagnosed are, in the majority of cases, simple continued fever, taking on a typhoid form but wanting in all the particulars of typhoid fever proper; and, I feel confident, was there an opportunity afforded for post-mortem examinations, they would be found wanting in the pathological changes peculiar to the disease.

There were 128 cases of pneumonia treated, with a loss of 45, almost 36 per cent., though not large when the condition of the patients at the time of entering the hospital is taken into consideration; a large majority of the cases are sick from three to ten days in camp before they are brought to the hospital. Such cases presenting bad symptoms, but still not necessarily of a fatal character, after a ride in an ambulance or wagon of three or five miles over a rough road, are placed beyond redemption. Stimulants and carb. ammonia may revive the vital spark, and the man live for several days, and occasionally, I am happy to say, has elasticity enough about his constitution to get well. As an evidence of the fatality caused by surrounding disadvantages, I have simply to refer to some ten or twelve cases of pneumonia in my nurses where every case has recovered, each one of them showing the good effects of antimony in the early stages of the disease.

Those sent from this place to general hospital, have been convalescents sent further back to make room for the sick. They have been South Carolinians and Mississippians, and were sent to Charlottesville and Warrenton.

The number of furloughs (47) is large for the number of patients; but when it is considered that all of the wounded—at least 60—from the battle of Drainesville, were here, that will be accounted for.

I may add that the two cases of erysipelas were purely idiopathic, and in the ward where all of the worst wounded were, there was quite a number of other cases there, arising from any little operations performed, such as removing a bullet or spicula of bone, but two patients operated on escaping; on one of those, I ligated the carotid artery, in the other amputation of the thigh was performed. The latter operation was performed three weeks since, and the same day a bullet was extracted from the shoulder, which immediately took on erysipelatous inflammation, whilst there has never been the slightest symptoms of it about the amputation. In several of these cases, and especially the idiopathic, the inflammation was not confined to the skin, but extended to the sub-cutaneous areolar tissue, forming what Dr. Stone, of New Orleans, says is different from erysipelas, and what he calls, "subcutaneous areolar inflammation," never running its course without suppuration, and occasionally to an enormous extent, invariably presenting typhoid (low) symptoms.

I am, Sir, your ob't Serv't,

J. F. BELL, P. A. C. S.,
Surgeon in Charge.

These examples might be multiplied, but these are believed to be sufficient to illustrate the experience of many Confederate surgeons, upon the intimate relations of Erysipelas in its origin and spread to such diseases as Hospital Gangrene which were known to be contagious.

On the other hand the armies were never so healthy, and the wounded were never so free from Erysipelas, as during the most active campaigns.

The army of General T. J. Jackson, (Stonewall), during its active campaign in the Valley of Virginia, was remarkably healthy, and the wounded, as I ascertained by an examination of the records of several of the largest hospitals, connected with the Department commanded by this distinguished soldier, were exempt to a great degree from both Erysipelas and Hospital Gangrene. This immunity was due to several causes, but chiefly to the active habits and good morale of his soldiers, to the comparatively abundant supplies of this rich country, and to the large and commodious hospitals established at Staunton and other eligible points in this elevated and healthy region. The truth of this assertion will be sustained in the following Sanitary Report of his Medical Director, Surgeon Hunter McGuire:

NEW MARKET, VA., April 15, 1862.

S. P. MOORE, Surgeon General, C. S. A.:

SIR: I have the honor to forward the consolidated report of sick and wounded, and the return of the Medical officers, serving in the Army of the Valley of Virginia for the month of March, 1862, (Maj. Gen'l Jackson's Command).

Though subjected to long, and sometimes forced marches, the health of this army was better during the month of March than during any other since its organization. It is a fact well known to Regimental Surgeons and Commanders, that the numbers reported sick during marches, even when they are long and fatiguing, provided the weather is clear and dry, is less than that which occurs when troops are stationary, and subjected to the ordinary duties of camp.

Towards the end of the month, recruits and drafted men were added to the regiments, and the amount of sickness increased, indeed the large proportion of those reported sick, belong to the men recently attached to the regiments, who are not yet inured to the hardships of a soldier's life. I enclose also a list of the killed and wounded of this army, in the engagement near Winchester, March 23, 1863. It numbers sixty-one killed, and three hundred and sixty-one wounded. Some of the latter were mortally wounded, and have since died, which increases the number of dead, as far as known, to eighty-eight, and proportionally reduces the number of wounded. One hundred and fifty-seven of the wounded were removed from the field, the rest fell into the hands of the enemy. It is gratifying to know that our dead were decently buried by the citizens of Winchester, and that our wounded have received every attention from the physicians and ladies of that place.

Very respectfully, your obedient servant,

HUNTER McGUIRE,
Medical Director, Army of Valley of Virginia.

Whilst we do not at all deny, that Erysipelas at times prevails as an epidemic, and appears to be produced by some general epidemic influence, and that in many cases the disease may be most plausibly accounted for, by sudden changes of atmospheric temperature, along with considerable moisture, together with derangement of the bowels, and the effects of particular articles of food; at the same time there are facts to show that this disease is at times, if not always contagious.

Neither would we be understood as insinuating, that instances of its transmission by contagion, are common in private practice, for isolated cases frequently occur in private families in which no member of the family and no nurse contracts the disease.

The origin and spread of Erysipelas in Hospitals, will depend upon the hygienic condition of the wards, and upon the state of the constitution of the patients.

Many of the Confederate Surgeons appeared to be aware of the dangers attending the indiscriminate use of sponges, dressings, and uncleansed wash bowls, when erysipelas was present in their wards. When wounds were cleansed with sponges or rags which had been used on erysipelatous patients, it was frequently observed that the disease appeared; and such propagation appeared to be clearly referable to the transference of the contagious matter.

It can be shown therefore that the evidence of contagion in Erysipelas rests upon nearly the same grounds as in the well known contagious diseases, scarlet fever, measles, and Typhus fever.

Many of the British Physicians and Surgeons, entertain but little doubt of the connexion, if not the identity of Erysipelas with Puerperal fever. Without entering into an extended examination of the facts upon which this view rests, it will be sufficient to recall the well known fact, that inoculation with the fluid of a female who had died of puerperal fever, is a most fatal source of diffuse cellular inflammation to the dissector.

Dr. George Gregory in his Lectures on the Eruptive Fevers, says that he had heard of a case, where vaccine matter taken from the arm of a child laboring under erysipelas, had communicated both diseases.

And finally Dr. Willan has testified, that if a person be inoculated with the fluid contained in the phlyctinae or vesicles of a genuine erysipelas, a red, painful, diffused swelling and inflammation analogous to erysipelas is produced.

This experiment has not as far as we are aware been repeated; and with such a direct demonstration of the possibility of communicating erysipelas by inoculation, we are at a loss to know upon what principles of reasoning, authors who have never performed a single experiment themselves, assume the right of setting aside the assertion of Dr. Willan.

By these facts therefore, as well as by those which occurred during the recent war, amongst the soldiers and citizens of the Confederate States, we are justified in drawing the conclusion, that it is possible to communicate the poison of Erysipelas, through the medinm of the vaccine matter.

The practical conclusion which we draw from this discussion, is that:

As far as possible soldiers, especially during long and fatiguing campaigns, and when crowded in hospitals and barracks, should be vaccinated with the lymph or vaccine virus from young healthy children. It is best, both in Civil and in Military practice, not to use the vaccine virus from the arms on soldiers, because their mode of life is an artificial one, to a great extent: a stereotyped life of restraint and hardship, and of great sameness of diet, and consequently a life liable to great excesses and irregularities of habits, and to great and sudden variations of health, as well as to slow and imperceptible deterioration of the nutritive fluids.

The quality of the vaccine virus, will depend in great measure upon the manner in which the nutrition of the body is per-for med. We use the word nutrition in its largest sense. Vaccine matter obtained from the arms of the feeble and often scorbutic convalescents of crowded civil and military hospitals, is wholly unfit for the propagation of the vaccine disease. Of all places, *civil and military Hospitals* are the *very last*, to which the profession should look for supplies of vaccine matter; and yet during the recent war, it was in the crowded hospitals that vaccination was most dilligently, perpetually, and indiscriminately performed. In these most destructive centres of contagious diseases, of Typhoid fever, Erysipelas, Hospital gangrene, and Pyæmia, the so-called vaccine matter passed from soldier to soldier in an endless round. Is there any marvel that under *such a system, enforced by military law*, the matter should have progressively deteriorated, and the accidents of vaccination, (Spurious vaccination) have become both common and serious?

SECTION VII.

Fresh and Dried Vaccine Lymph and Scabs from Patients suffering with Secondary or Constitutional Syphilis, at the time, and during the progress of Vaccination and the Vaccine Disease.

We examined at different times, during the progress of the recent war, and also had under treatment, various skin affections, which presented the characters of the cutaneous diseases, characteristic of secondary Syphilis, which were directly traceable to impure vaccine virus. I saw several cases in which enlarged buboes in the axilla and groin accompanied the peculiar skin affection induced by impure vaccine matter. No such results followed vaccination as performed by myself or immediately under my direction during the war: these accidents were avoided in my civil and military practice, by adhering rigidly to the rule of using the lymph from the arms of healthy children and infants: the opportunity therefore did not present itself of observing and carfully noting the disease in its first stages. The cases resembling constitutional Syphilis and which were said to have resulted directly from vaccination, which came under my observation and treatment, were as a general rule of long standing, and had been collected from different hospitals, and from various regiments, serving in widely separated districts.

In the summer of 1863, I examined a large number, and if my memory is correct, over two hundred cases of severe skin affections and general constitutional derangement resulting from vaccination, in the large hospitals in and around Richmond, Virginia. In these cases, as well as in those examined in other parts of Virginia, South Carolina, and Georgia, great difficulty was experienced in tracing the impure matter to a definite source, that is to the point at which it became contaminated or deteriorated. I do not wish to be understood as asserting or insinuating that this large number of cases presented the symptoms of secondary Syphilis: so far from this it appeared to me that those cases which presented the most complete resemblance with constitutional Syphilis were not as numerous as those which were clearly referable to scorbutic and other deranged conditions of the system induced by fatigue, exposure and bad diet.

During the progress of the war, the subject of the relation of vaccination to constitutional Syphilis, engaged my most anxious thought, and I had determined to make it a special subject of investigation in the Field and General Hospitals, immediately upon the completion of my investigations upon Typhoid fever, Malarial fever, Small Pox, Hospital Gangrene, and Pyæmia, believing that a correct solution of this difficult and important question was to be obtained only by a personal examination of the cases as they arose in the regiments serving in the field, and by a careful collection and examination of the testimony of the regimental Surgeons and Assistant Surgeons. From experience gained in other investigations in the Field and General Hospitals, I was well aware that such labors required much time and were beset with many difficulties. From the terrible drain upon the Confederate States for men, the hospitals and convalescent camps were subjected to the most rigid scrutiny, and all men not absolutely disabled from every kind of duty, were at the earliest possible moment transferred to clerical and light duty in the Quartermaster, Commissary, Medical and Purveying departments. From the great disparity of numbers, and from the immense extent of country in which the operations were conducted, the Confederate troops were in perpetual motion. The same soldiers, in the course of a few months, conducted fatiguing campaigns which extended over entire States, and fought bloody and desperate battles with superior forces in localities separated by hundreds of miles. Whole armies that had been victorious at some remote portion of the border, or of the Atlantic and Gulf coasts, were suddenly transported by railroad, across the entire Confederacy, to take their immediate part, without rest, in the bloody battles of the mountains of Tennessee and in the valleys of Virginia. These difficulties were experienced to a greater or less degree by every medical officer who undertook the investigation of this subject; and it has been rendered still more obscure, by the sudden manner in which the struggle terminated, and by the loss of the most extensive and valuable reports on file in the Surgeon General's office at Richmond.

I have sought to remedy, in a small degree, these defects, by addressing inquiries to a large number of those who formerly occupied positions in the medical service favorable for the investigation of the causes of the accidents following vaccination. It must be confessed that up to the present time, the replies received to these inquiries, have been wanting in that full and accurate detail of individual cases, which is so necessary to the proper solution of the question, whether the lymph or scab of a vaccine vesicle may, beside its peculiar virus, contain another infectious principle, as that of Syphilis.

The affirmative of this question was held by many, both in civil and military practice; and a number of the Confederate Surgeons, boldly took the ground that secondary Syphilis could be communicated along with the vaccine virus, and especially when the dried scabs were employed. In the records upon this subject, which we examined in the Surgeon General's office in the Confederate Capital, this view was clearly announced. Several of these reports had been prepared in accordance with a direct order issued by the Surgeon General, directing a careful investigation into the origin and causes of spurious vaccination. The history, and results of a portion of the investigations ordered by Dr. Moore, are given in the following letter from my friend, Professor S. M. Bemiss, M. D., now of the Medical Department of the University of Louisiana. Dr. Bemiss enjoyed most extended opportunities for the investigation of this subject not only during his connection with the Army of Northern Virginia, but also during his efficient service as Assistant Medical Director of the Army of Tennessee.

NEW ORLEANS, November 21, 1866.

PROF. JOSEPH JONES, University of Nashville;
MY DEAR SIR:
Yours of the 9th instant, reached me to-day. I regret that I can furnish you no information likely to be of service to you in the investigation you have undertaken. During the month of March, 1863, while connected with the army of Northern Virginia, Medical Director Guild was so impressed with the importance of this affection that he ordered a committee of investigation into the extent of its prevalence, its causes and nature. I think the committee limited their inspections to those regiments only whose medical officers had reported the presence of this "Spurious vaccination." The committee consisted of Surgeons R. J. Breckinridge, now of Houston, Texas, Herndon, of Fredericksburg, Virginia, and ———, of North Carolina. I was not officially connected with the committee, but accompanied it from motives of professional interest. I kept many valuable notes in reference to the appearance of the ulcers and their history; but at the close of the war my camp chest was lost and with it all my MSS. My recollections are that the cases of spurious vaccination were most numerous in the 12th and 16th Ga. Regiments. In one of those regiments we found over one hundred cases of ulcerated arms and hands, and in many instances extending to the body and lower extremities. In one of these regiments the historical connection with Syphilis was most conclusive. They had all been vaccinated from the arm of a comrade of very dissolute habits, who had just returned from a leave of absence. This soldier was at this time in camp and presented unmistakable evidences of Syphilis. I do not think I err when I state that there was no chancre on the penis, but we rested our opinion of the existence of Syphilis upon the characteristic sore throat and eruption, and his confessions as to the recent existence of chancre. He had just returned from some little village in Georgia, and informed us that a physician practicing there, I think by the name of Russell, had taken matter from his arm and inserted it into the arms of a large number of young persons in his neighborhood. I regret that I cannot recall the names of the medical officers of these regiments, so that you might address them letters of enquiry. The "vaccination" in all these cases was done by the soldiers themselves and not by their medical officers, consequently, acting upon the popular idea that the larger the sore the more complete is the protection, they selected the worst sores for the propagation of the virus. I remember that the committee agreed

with regard to the worst of these ulcers, that their appearance and progress were so analogous to syphilides that they did not hesitate to class them as such. The usual treatment for Syphilis did not *cure or benefit these cases with any marked uniformity.* I think we find a ready explanation of this observation in the condition of constitution and circumstances under which the treatment was instituted, poor diet, scurvy and camp life. During my long service in the western army I saw much of this form of disease, and in the majority of cases failed to connect it with Syphilis, either as it respects history or characteristics. I treated one case in which the manifestations were decidedly syphilitic, but the soldier had suffered from constitutional disease in bad form for some year or more previously. In brief, toward the conclusion of the war I abandoned my previous opinion that *all* such cases were true syphilides, and was willing to admit that some of them could not be classed with those affections either by history, characteristics, or progress, and that we must refer them to the introduction of a poison differing from Syphilis, or to some peculiar constitutional crasis which determined the character of the sores. I refer you to the following gentlemen: Dr. L. Guild, Mobile, Alabama; Dr. James C. Mullens, ——, S. C.; Dr. R. P. Bateman, Memphis; Dr. B. M. Wible, Louisville.

Very respectfully, &c., S. M. BEMISS.

Professor Paul F. Eve, M.D., of the Medical Department of the University of Nashville, as will be seen in the following quotation from his article "On the Health of the Southern Army," believes that Syphilis may be transmitted by vaccination.

"*Syphilis in Connection with Vaccination.*—From all I have heard and read on the transmissibility of Syphilis by vaccination, the question, from the evidence already accumulated, would appear decided in the affirmative. While I have *seen* nothing confirming this opinion, yet I do know that cases did occur in Richmond, Va., said to be corroborative of it, and that Medical officers in the Southern service were specially cautioned as to the source whence vaccine matter was derived. Since my return to Nashville, I find that the opinion obtains among the Surgeons of the United States Army, that in some instances syphilitic diseases have been definitely traced to the insertion of vaccine matter. My colleague, Dr. Briggs, called my attention recently to a case of this kind, of the source of which he entertains no doubt. I failed to see it, as the patient had left for the Hot Springs of Arkansas. When told that he had the secondary symptoms of Syphilis, he replied that was impossible, as he never yet had contracted the primary, though confessing that he was almost daily exposed to it. Two other physicians were consulted as to the affection, and from this history of the case were inclined to the belief of the patient, but stated it looked like venereal. It was subsequently ascertained that this person had been vaccinated from a girl of the town who labored under constitutional Syphilis. Not only was the arm in this instance made very sore, but buboes formed in the axilla, followed by ulcerations in the throat, copper blotches in the skin, nodes, &c.

"The possibility of communicating Syphilis by vaccination, was agitated in Italy as far back as 1846; and the transmissibility of this unfortunate contamination was there definitely admitted in 1861, by a committee elected at a Medical Congress at Acqui in Piedmont, at which it was believed that numerous cases had occurred in both children and adults, who had been vaccinated. The names of Pacchiotti, Parola, Ponza, Tassani, of Milan, who I met there in charge of a large hospital after the battles of Magenta and Solferino, in 1859, De Kalt, Hubner, &c., vouch for the accuracy of this report. The transmission of (syphilitic) disease has also been maintained by Lecoq, Rollet of Lyons, and particularly by Vennois in the Archives Générales de Medicine of Paris, 1860; and on this point, the admission of Dr. D. F. Condie, long known to occupy the front rank in the profession, and who has done so much for its literature, deserves serious consideration; and he publishes these words in a recent number of the American Journal of Medical Sciences:

"'Let it be strongly impressed upon the mind of every physician, lest in his attempt to guard the system against one formidable malady, he inoculate with another, more insidious in its operations, but not less destructive.'

"As to the consentaneous presence of two constitutional diseases in the same patient, and the contagiousness of secondary symptoms of Syphilis, it is sufficient for us to state that at a recent meeting of the Academy of Medicine in Paris, the the report from a committee, on which M. M. Velpeau and Ricord served, (than whom it may be safely asserted two better names for this very purpose never existed in the annals of the profession), decided both these questions in the affirmative."

Dr. O. Kratz, in the following report to the Surgeon General, on vaccination, originally published in the July number of the Confederate States Medical and Surgical Journal, (vol. i., 1864, p. 104), supported the view that Secondary Syphilis could be communicated through the medium of the Vaccine Virus.

On Vaccination and Variolous Diseases. By O. Kratz, Surgeon, P. A. C. S.

The following remarks on Vaccination and Variolous Diseases have been suggested to me from my own experience. Spurious Vaccine and its deleterious influence on Vaccination, seem to me worthy of further investigation, as a subject hitherto not sufficiently appreciated.

In order to define my stand-point, let me state, at the outset, that Liebig's Theory of Fermentation is till now, the best to explain the phenomena of vaccination, and that all the anomalies occurring, may be best elucidated by this hypothesis. At the same time I do not feel warranted in subscribing blindly to it; but I think we have not any better as yet, and I simply adopt it in the same manner as I would have to conform to the atomic theory in treating about chemistry.

In vaccinating a subject we introduce, then, the yeast, the virus, into the circulation, to produce the fermentation and its result, the scab. If there is a certain substance in the system for the virus to reäct upon, the scab will be formed and the subject is vaccinated. If, on the contrary, this substance is entirely deficient or modified in some way or other, no scab, or an imperfect one, will be the result.

With very few exceptions, the good vaccine matter, will produce a normal scab on the subject never vaccinated before. The reäcting matter in the system is eliminated, and by this process the liability to the infection of small-pox rendered impossible or greatly diminished. Possibly, in a long interval of time, this matter may be re-organized in the body, but never to its original state. I say never, because such a subject may be attacked by varioloides, but never by variola.

If this re-acting matter is re-organized as nearly as possible to its original state, the second vaccination will produce a scab also, but never a perfect one. It may be perfect for the protection of the individual on whom it appears, but it offers no guarantee for re-vaccination on other subjects. I call this a pseudo-scab. This scab may yet retain much of the original fermenting property, but not the same as the genuine. If this virus is used again for re-vaccination of an individual, its product will offer again less guarantees of being protective. Continuing in this manner, the scab will finally contain nothing but common suppurative matter—pus—as if taken from any other suppurating place in the body. The germ of the scab itself will be more or less modified and deviating from its normal structure.

As I have no book of reference on the subject, I quote the following from memory:

Some years ago, the Academy of Medicine in Paris investigated very closely the fact, if syphilis could be transferred by vaccination. The result obtained by repeated and most direct experiments was, that it could not be communicated by transmission of genuine Vaccine Virus, from one individual to another, affected with syphilis in any of its stages. Liebig's explanatory theory of fermentation holds good here. The Vaccine Virus will re-act only on certain substances in the system and ignore others entirely. We know, at the same time, that matter from a syphilitic suppurating surface will reproduce syphilitic symptoms on another subject.

I have had occasion to observe several well defined cases of Rupia Syphilitica produced solely by vaccination. Other respectable Surgeons, worthy of implicit belief, from their scientific attainments, have noticed the same and similar facts repeatedly.

These subjects had never had Syphilis before, otherwise the inference would be doubtful or worthless altogether. Therefore, instead of having had vaccine virus inserted, they have been inoculated with Syphilis.

I have seen one case, where the product of the vaccination was Surpetigo rodeus, a frightful disease of, I believe, a cancerous character. Some cases had herpes excedens as the result of vaccination on their arm.

The syphilitic cases had been treated for other cutaneous diseases without any material amelioration. The mercurial treatment removed the symptoms at once.

I have never seen anomalous results from vaccination if the following precaution was strictly adhered to: The vaccine matter used was taken from a healthy infant, never vaccinated before.

The indiscriminate vaccination and re-vaccination from arm to arm has been, in my opinion, the principal cause of the deterioration of the vaccine virus, and of producing cutaneous diseases from vaccination. A second cause may be found in the fact, that the virus used is old and too rarely regenerated by passing it through the cow. Cow virus will fail only 1 in 100; good common virus will fail 3 in 100, if I remember right.—*Confederate States Medical and Surgical Journal,* July, 1864.

The testimony of Doctor Wm. F. Fuqua, of Virginia, formerly Surgeon of the 7th Florida Regiment, C. S. A.. is clear and decided. Fifty-two Confederate soldiers, who had been inoculated with virus from the arm of a sailor who was laboring under Syphilis, presented the characteristic symptoms of constitutional Syphilis, as abcesses in the axillary glands, pain in the limbs and joints, sensation of dryness and ulceration in the throats, buboes, coppery colored spots, and loss of hair, and they were only relieved by syphilitic treatment. If these results of vaccination had been due to a depressed and scorbutic state of the blood, the syphilitic mercurial treatment would have greatly aggravated the diseased condition.

On the Communicability of Syphilis by Vaccination. By WM. M. FUQUA, M.D.. Appomatox County, Virginia.

On assuming charge of the Seventh Florida Regiment, late C. S. A., as Medical officer, I found fifty-two men who had been recently vaccinated, suffering from severe ulcers on their arms, at the site of vaccination. Some of these ulcers had scabbed, and to all appearances seemed to promise a speedy "return to duty." There were others, varying in size from that of a quarter of a dollar to that of a Mexican dollar. Their edges were hard, shining, and everted; in some few cases they were undermined. An ashy coloured slough covered their base, which was from time to time cast off. This, however, was not always a genuine slough, but a tenacious grey and partially organized exudation. These ulcers were offensive, and discharged pus freely. The redness circumscribing them, was limited, the limb but little swollen, and the pain of a burning, stinging character. In many instances, the lymphatic vessels were much inflamed, and the axillary glands, in each case, were more or less affected. Many of these patients complained of pain in their limbs; there was some febrile excitement, and their appetites had been much impaired. Having thus briefly described these ulcers, it may not be improper to remark upon the hygienic condition of the regiment.

At this time, it was doing duty at Knoxville, in the department of East Tennessee, and was quartered a mile from town, upon soil which had been previously occupied by troops, who had left the encampment in no praiseworthy condition. To the south, southwest, and west, passed the Holston river. The general health of the command was bad—the sick list comprising one-seventh of the command. The prevailing diseases were the malarial fevers and acute diarrhœa.

The first part of the treatment of these cases, consisted in their removal to a more cleanly and healthful locality; cleanliness of person and clothing was enjoined also. General directions were given as regards diet, and of maintaining their bowels in proper condition. The second part of the treatment was the local application of astringents in the milder cases, and escharotics, varying from the mildest kind to that of the most potential, in conjunction with the astringent lotions in the severe ones. Under this regimen, some few improved; none, however, recovered; by far the greater number grew worse. Abcesses now began to form in the axillary glands; pain in the limbs and joints increased in severity; there was a sensation of dryness in the throats of many, which was speedily followed by ulceration. Our apprehensions were now fully awakened; each day we inquired more and more diligently for some new symptom which might be diagnostic. Coppery coloured spots now appeared upon two; the hair began to fall off in a third, and it was not a week before a syphilitic bubo, in its incipient stage, appeared in another. Heretofore, these cases had been denominated "spurious vaccination." Spurious they were, in one sense; but specific in another, in the strictest acceptation of the term.

It is hardly requisite for me to state, that these cases were placed upon syphilitic treatment, and we had the satisfaction, in comparitively short time, of seeing the greater number of them returned to duty. A few were sent to the General Hospital, one of whom died.

In conclusion, let me remark, that having mentioned to Dr. Frank Ramsey, then, Medical Director of the Department, the nature of these cases, he requested me to make a report in detail concerning them, which was done, and in all probability found its way to the late Surgeon General's office.

Upon inquiry, it was definitely ascertained, that the virus for inoculating these patients was obtained from a sailor, on the coast of Florida, who labored under primary Syphilis at the time of vaccination.—*Richmond Journal of Medicine and Surgery*, June, 1866.

The following article by Dr. Frank A. Ramsey, of Memphis, Tennessee, contains an argument for the possibility of the transmission of Syphilis by vaccination, although its author does not feel justified in supporting this opinion in "a strictly professional disquisition." In a letter from Dr. Ramsey to myself, accompanying this paper, dated Memphis, November 15, 1866, he says: "The subject has occasioned me much thought, and incidentally some research, being on the watch for anything, however remote, at all applicable to the question. But I cannot say that I have formed any definite views regarding the question involved."

Abnormalities of Vaccination. By FRANK A. RAMSEY, M.D., Medical Director of the (Quondam) C. S. A.

It is after conference, regarded as proper for the following letter to be published. The subject matter of which it treats, was one of exceeding importance and interest, almost from the incipiency of the intestine strife, in the Southern States, but has not yet had, in the professional periodicals, any exhibition of the attention it elicited, or any declarations of results of observation, or of investigation.

I do not deem it necessary to defend now, the course of thought taken in the letter, written under the peculiar circumstances connected with the period at which it bears date. It has, however, a reference to a particular opinion, which I would not at any time, or under any circumstances, support in a strictly professional disquisition; that opinion had been hastily expressed, in the midst of official business, and for the purpose of producing a particular effect, which I honestly judged to be proper and best in the exigency.

Effects very nearly resembling rupia, followed vaccination, with presumptively pure virus, in so many instances, as induced the Surgeon General, to appoint medical officers connected with the Southern army, to the duty of tracing, if any, the connection between syphilis and vaccinia; and the prosecution of this duty gave occasion to the letter, now presented in the hope that it will lead others to record their observation, experiences and reflections, on the same subject; and with the intention on the part of the writer himself, under other and more favorable conditions to give the subject further consideration:

MEDICAL DIRECTOR'S OFFICE
ABINGDON, VIRGINIA, March 20, 1864.

DOCTOR:—Your note, of March the eleventh, informing me, that you had been appointed "chairman of a committee on the relation of vaccination to Syphilis," and making reference to my "report of last year," and asking me for "any further information relative to Spurious vaccination," has been received; and I take the first opportunity, offered in the performance of official duties, to reply.

I have no facts, which have occurred within the field of my own observation, directly relating to the subject, as stated by you; but, with your permission, will continue writing, until I have given you something of the operation of my mind, occasioned by your note.

I thank you for the honor you have done me, in preferring the request, and in the reference you have made to, I presume, a letter written by me, to a Surgeon at Chattanooga, a copy of which I deemed proper to forward to the Surgeon General. That letter was written, as I now write to you, *currente calamo*, and though I preserved a copy, it was left at Knoxville, and has doubtless fallen into the possession of the enemy. I am, therefore, prevented from making reference to it, as I am debarred from any ability to consult authority, or to refresh my memory, as I should, and would do, if differently situated. But, if I correctly remember, the letter was not of such a character, as to convey an idea, that the observations were of cases of Spurious vaccination. Indeed, the basis of the letter was furnished by observations of results, or effects following the introduction, or inoculation of vaccine virus undoubtedly pure. And though the results or exhibits were in their course, certainly not such as ordinarily present from vaccination, or as are usually recognized as essentially cow-pox; yet observations were not sufficiently numerous, or continued for a time long enough, to determine whether any, or the same degree of immunity from small-pox was occasioned in subjects thus affected, as in those who presented the ordinary course of the cow-pox disease. There were, however, practitioners of medicine, who were esteemed, in communities in which they labored, as capable observers, who affirmed that these subjects were as free from liability to small-pox, as those in whose economies the vaccine disease had exhibited nothing unusual, in deviation from its regular course. If, then, the scab was undoubtedly a pure vaccine scab, and the effect was perfect, or relatively perfect, immunity from small-pox, notwithstanding there was nothing observed from the application of the virus, until the production of the ultimate effect, at all like vaccine disease in progress, the disease, I think, cannot properly be termed spurious. To be spurious, the vaccine virus must not be in the scab, or the effect must be an absence of any protective energy having been impressed on the economy into which the scab had been introduced. Varioloid consists of exhibits in course, differing from variola in course, yet no one, I presume, would feel himself justified in terming it spurious small-pox, because it is known to proceed from small-pox virus, will communicate small-pox, and leaves the economy it has affected, impressed with immunity from a future attack of small-pox. Varioloid is, then, not spurious small-pox, but small-pox modified in its exhibits in progress, through an economy previously impressed by the operation of the virus of cow-pox. Here the modifying cause is known.

So by analogy, the cases which gave occasion to my letter of last year, were, each, an instance of modified cow-pox. The matter was obtained from Nashville, Tenn., from Atlanta, Ga., and from Richmond, Virginia, from Surgeons of reliability, and the same results were observed to follow upon the introduction of the several matters, in some instances regular vaccinia, in others abnormal exhibitions; indeed, in many an approximation to the regular exhibition of original poison from cow matter, could not be discovered. And professional men, who were not destitute of reputation for capacity, affirmed, on the strength of observations sufficient to satisfy them, that the economies thus affected, were impressed with immunity from small-pox, as though they had passed through cow-pox in its regular exhibitions.

True, to make complete the analogy I have instituted, it remains to establish by experiment, that true vaccinia in its regular exhibitions, in one instance, or more, can be produced by the inoculation of matter from one of these economies. Which experiment, however, I will leave to some one with more curiosity and temerity than I have, feeling satisfied myself, that they were cases of modified cow-pox. But in these instances, the modifying cause is unknown. It must, however, have obtained an union with cow-pox matter, in its passage through an economy peculiarly affected, and, therefore, resided in the scab, not altered from its ordinary physical appearance, because, as yet, not sufficiently imbued with the acquired and modifying contagion. Or, it must have been a peculiar condition of the individual economies, into which the vaccine virus was introduced. Or, it must have been telluric or celestial relationships sustained by the particular persons affected; or, as Sydenham's comprehensive term is applicable in giving expression to such relationships—" the epidemic constitution."

In my previous letter, I believe, I advanced this last as sufficient to account for the abnormalities which had been observed. It is the more easily assumed, and probably the more easily sustained position. I will, however, not undertake to defend it here, for, notwithstanding my great respect to the "epidemic constitution," when I am at the bedside of a patient, I can, when I am reflecting, readily comprehend, that either one or all the positions may be defended, as the source of cause in its influence modifying cow-pox.

Will vaccine virus become possessed of capacity acquired in its passage through an economy peculiarly diseased, to propagate such disease in other economies? The question thus stated, will, in some degree, embrace the relation of vaccination to Syphilis.

Whether there is truth in the doctrine which has been promulgated, that two distinct contagious diseases cannot exist at the same time, in the same economy, it is not amiss to make reference to it here; for if it is not true, the fact does not justify the assumption, that two poisonous causes cannot be introduced into an economy at the same moment, one having the office of vehicle for the other—does not justify an assumption, that two poisonous causes in the same economy, at the same time, can occasion no modification, each of the other, or the one of the other- and if it is true, the fact or modification is at once established. More directly assertive of the virus acquiring a modifying capacity, even to the complete destruction of original physical appearances, and exhibitions of effects, is the idea suggested during the year 1800, by Richard Dunning, Surgeon, Plymouth-Dock, that " the vaccine disease, united with some other virus, may have afforded the more active affection of variola." Dunning's reviewer, from whom I received my information, says, " the hint deserves some attention, as a point of speculation, which cannot be subjected to the test of experiment."

I only make reference to it as an assertion made long ago, that one virus may be modified by another; for I do not regard the poisons of variola and vaccinia as being at all identical. This, I think, is evident, if there is truth in the following statement: Small-pox and varioloid will produce small-pox, but never cow-pox. Cow-pox will produce cow-pox, but never small-pox or varioloid. Cow-pox will prevent the occurence of small-pox, or mitigate its severity, and lessen its mortality in the human economy. Small-pox having occurred in the human economy, is not preventive of cow-pox, if its poison be introduced by inoculation. Cow-pox, reproduced in the human system, inserted into the teat of the cow, will produce cow-pox. Small-pox, similarly introduced into brute animals, will not produce small-pox. This last assertion is made by Wm. Woodville, M. D., London, 1800, and by others, perhaps before, and several times repeated, since, and within the past two years, medical officers in the service have attempted, at Greenville, Tenn., to occasion small-pox in a cow, in one instance, and in a calf in another instance, using matter taken from a case of confluent small-pox, then under treatment, and inserting it under the cuticle, and introducing it into the stomachs, mixed with food, and without any bad effects whatever, or any disturbance of the health of the animals. I am aware, that observations have been published, seemingly different from this, but there is a want of explicitness in connection with their relation, which justifies a doubt of authenticity. But this, if you please, by way of parenthesis.

The most insidious of contagious poisons affecting the human economy is, probably, the syphilitic. It has, doubtless, occurred to almost every practitioner, to observe cases in which the subjects were known to have been treated for Syphilis, and afterwards, to have exhibited for many, very many years, entire health, when occasion, known or unknown, presented, and they offered themselves for treatment, affected with disease which the physician pronounced to be syphilitic, and which could not be cured, except by the administration of anti-syphilitic agents. The poison had remained latent, or dormant for these many years, only awaiting circumstances or conditions, favorable to the exercise of its capacity to affect. I had under my charge, for twenty years, a family, the children of which were generally healthy, whose father was treated for Syphilis from the age of nineteen to twenty-four; since which, he has enjoyed good health seemingly, in every particular. His children, however, were frequently attacked with illness, deemed sufficient to require my professional attention. No odds, how simple the attack, even though, when I first called, the evidences were nothing more than those of slight catarrh, I have never known them yield or mitigate, until one dose, or more, of a mercurial—generally calomel—had been administered. This I have ascribed to the presence in their economies of the syphilitic poison derived from their father, and exerting an influence retarding healthy developments, or preventing the disappearance of symptoms of diseased action, not in themselves syphilitic. The cases cited in "Montgomery on Pregnancy," bear well on this point. A woman married a man with latent constitutional Syphilis. She became infected, which was first exhibited at conception, or in miscarriage, followed by secondary symptoms of Syphilis. A woman contracted Syphilis, was treated and recovered. A considerable time afterward she married. One, two, or three children were born, all affected with Syphilis. The husband died, and the woman married again, a healthy man; and to this husband, children were born, and all died, except one, affected with Syphilis; the exception had mercury and recovered. One of the children communicated Syphilis to the woman by whom it was nursed.

But the insidiousness of this contagion is more strongly exhibited in another case, cited by Montgomery. A woman, whose husband had constitutional Syphilis, gave birth to a child; which died with Syphilis in two months, the mother remaining wholly free from any exhibits of the affection. This husband died, and she married again, a healthy man. Four years after the former birth, she was delivered of a child, which, in a few months, presented the same syphilitic apprarances manifested by the child of the first husband.

If these instances are, as observers affirm them to be, true, how little effort does it require for the mind to conceive the probability of a vaccine scab, having acquired the capacity from an economy, affected with Syphilis, to propagate that disease? If a woman can remain in health, after sexual congress with a man affected with latent constitutional Syphilis, and yet years afterward, give birth to syphilitic children, begotten by a healthy man, it is within the bounds of legitimate assumption, to affirm that syphilitic exhibits may be manifested in an economy, by the introduction of vaccine matter, taken from an economy tainted with Syphilis, even though it is in that system in latency, and had never been developed.

Two of the cases which gave occasion to my letter of last year, were ladies whose husbands occupied prominent and responsible positions in society. Neither the husbands or wives were at all under suspicion of immoral taint. The wives were vaccinated, and for many months were affected with ulcerations, which, under other circumstances, would have been, without hesitation, pronounced to be syphilitic rupia. They came under the care of Act. As't. Surgeon Meadows, then, as now, in charge of Small-pox Hospitals in this department. He put them on the use of bi-chloride of mercury, and they both recovered in ten or fifteen days.

Permit me to summarize. Two contagions may be introduced into the human economy at the same moment of time, and connected with the same vehicle; or, one contagion may be the vehicle of another, and each may exert its own ultimate effects, the intermediate effects being the exhibitions of but one or the other of the contagions having made impression, or, the intermediate effects may be the exhibitions of one poison, which, having passed their course, the intermediate effects exhibiting the presence of the other poison, supervene and pass their course. Syphilis and vaccine. Two contagions, may respectively modify each other. An illustration does not occur to me. One contagion may modify another, and while it is itself not subjected to a modifying influence, exerted by the one it has modified, it may be modified by another contagion. Cow-pox and small-pox, cow-pox and Syphilis. The introduction of one contagion into an economy, may arouse another, which has remained dormant or latent, and unsuspected. Cow pox and Syphilis.

An item relative to the treatment of Small-pox:—Act. As't. Surgeon Meadows, in two cases of Small-pox, occurring in children, employed croton oil, applying it on the third and fourth day of the active fever, to the breast, producing full and confluent pustulation. The immediate effect was, certainly unpleasant—very considerable cerebral disturbance, evidently, in its intensity, ascribable to the croton oil pustulation: but he is convinced, that the course of the disease was shortened two-thirds, desquamation beginning on the seventh day, instead of during the second week; and that the eruption was one half less than it would have been under other circumstances. He has, also, practiced opening each pimple, just as it assumed the vesicular character; with the effect, he believes, of expediting the process, desquamation occurring one third the time sooner than usual.

I have written, Doctor, hurriedly, but I hope that I have not been so rapid, as to have failed wholly of interesting you, at least for the moment.

Very respectfully, your obedient servant,

FRANK A. RAMSEY,
Surgeon and Medical Director, P. A. C. S.

To JAMES BOLTON, M, D.,
Chairman committee on the Relation of Vaccina to Syphilis, Richmond, Va.—*The Medical and Surgical Monthly,*—May, 1866—p. 140-147.

Dr. Crawford, of Greeneville, Tenn., was able to trace the impure virus which produced indurated ulcers and constitutional symptoms, to a single individual, and the disease thus disseminated by inoculation, yielded to the remedies best adapted to the treatment of syphilis.

GREENVILLE, TENN., Jan. 27, 1867.

PROF. JOSEPH JONES, M.D.:

DEAR SIR:—Having seen, in the January Number of the "NASHVILLE JOURNAL OF MEDICINE AND SURGERY," a circular letter addressed by you to the Surgeons of the late Confederate Army, instituting inquiries upon *"Spurious Vaccination,"* I desire to respond to your inquiries, and to communicate those facts in my possession, which may throw light upon this subject, which is fraught with so much interest to science and humanity.

During the winter of 1862 and 1863, I was "Surgeon in charge" of the "Madison Hospital" (Confederate) at this place, during which time over one thousand patients came under my charge. Small-pox made its appearance in the Hospital 15th November, 1862. In anticipation of the appearance of the disease, I had some time previous, procured a fresh supply of genuine vaccine virus by vaccinating some healthy children. In this way I had kept a fresh supply on hand since 1856. That is by vaccinating some healthy child every few months. I immediately ordered all patients then in hospital (350) to be vaccinated, both those that had been, as well as those that had not previously been vaccinated. The matter took well upon all who had not been vaccinated, and imperfectly in some cases that had been vaccinated. A "Pest-house" was established, and the infected, as soon as the nature of the disease was manifested, removed at once to it. The disease did not extend to the patients in hospital; but from time to time patients were admitted, many of whom proved to be suffering with variola. But in no single instance was the disease communicated to those that had been recently vaccinated or re-vaccinated, and but six cases of varioloid occurred out of the 850 patients, all of whom had been exposed to the contagion of small-pox. There was great alarm, both among citizens and soldiers; for the small-pox cases were exceedingly fatal, owing to the want of proper comforts and attention. Out of 90 cases, 40 proved fatal. Neither the citizen nor soldier was satisfied of his immunity from danger, unless he could make a *"sore"* of some sort upon his arm. Consequently vaccination was perseveringly sought from the ugliest and foulest looking ulcers. The idea being with the masses, that vaccination loses its effects after a few years, and must be renewed: if a sore was not produced by matter from one arm, another was sought. This state of things continued without any mischievous effects until about the first of January, 1863, when Col. Clayton, then Commander of the Post at this place, who had been on leave of absence some weeks in North Carolina, returned with an ugly looking ulcer upon his right arm which was reported to be the genuine matter. The cry of *eureka* was raised, and it was not long until dozens, both citizens and soldiers, had this matter inserted into their arms. From this dates the history of "Spurious Vaccination." Col. Clayton had been successfully vaccinated some years before; but so soon as it was known that we were in the midst of the most loathsome of all diseases, I re-vaccinated him twice with genuine virus, but without effect. What the history of the case was from which he received the infectious matter, I never learned, for the Colonel could not find out. Col. Clayton was about 21 years of age, sanguine temperament, and in excellent health at the time he received the infectious matter into his arm. The ulcers I regarded at the time, and still regard, as caused by inoculation with *syphilitic virus*. The cases ran an indefinite course of from three weeks to six months, and yielded only to *Blue Mass, Iodide Potassium*, internally, and *Sul. Cupri.* externally. Some cases taken in their incipiency, yielded in a few days to the external treatment alone.

It is proper to state that there was no tendency to scorbutic disease among either soldiers or citizens, and the infectious matter was equally as severe among the citizens as soldiers. The hospital was well provided with everything calculated to promote comfort and health. The patients were in good houses, had plenty of clothing, and rations in abundance, such as fresh meats, fruits, potatoes, cabbage, &c. There was no scarcity of these things in this country at that time, and what the Government did not provide, the citizens supplied with a liberal hand.

This "Spurious Vaccination" yielded no protection whatever from variola. I have seen more than a dozen cases of variola occur where there were large ulcers from this spurious virus, the patients thinking they were protected from the disease by such "*sores.*" The spurious matter would take effect in all cases and all sorts of constitutions.

About this time orders were issued from Surgeon General Moore to procure fresh vaccine virus through the cow, I tried the experiment three times without succeeding. First on a cow seven years old, with a calf six months old. Then a young heifer two years old, and finally the calf. I inserted the matter in the teats, nose, ears and various parts of the skin, but never succeeded in getting a crust. Finally I fed the calf on the dried scabs mixed with its food, but it died without yielding me the much sought for treasure.

In August, 1863, the Confederate Army evacuated East Tennessee, and in September, 1863, the Federal Army took possession and held for a time. That army under Gen. Burnsides was composed of new recruits, made up mostly of six months volunteers, many of whom had not been in the service three months. This same disease was among them. This army was abundantly supplied with anti-scorbutics, and fed with a liberal hand, and had never been exposed to hardships.

My best wishes for your success in your undertaking.

Yours sincerely, S. P. CRAWFORD.

If such accidents had been confined entirely to the Confederate Army, or to the period of the war, when the citizens were to a greater or less extent subjected to unusual privations, and to the action of the most depressing causes, the views of those who denied emphatically the possibility of transmitting the poison of constitutional syphilis by the process of vaccination, would receive at least a show of support from the apparent dependence of the abnormal phenomena accompanying the vaccine disease, upon the depressed and deranged states of the system, induced by improper nutrition and physical causes.

It happened, however, that a large number of cases, which were referred by both citizens and physicians, to the contamination of the vaccine virus with the syphilitic poison, occurred in the quiet manufacturing community of Graniteville, after the close of the war.

Under the kind, liberal and efficient management of the intelligent head of the Graniteville Manufacturing Company, the operatives enjoyed comfortable dwellings and abundant supplies of nutritious and wholesome food. This class of the population of South Carolina were perhaps, more favorably situated, as to subsistance and support, than the great majority of the citizens of South Carolina, whose dwellings and barns had been laid in ashes, and whose social and agricultural system, the growth of centuries, had been so completely overturned, as to convert, without warning, the richest into the poorest.

The following report of Dr. W. F. Percival, of Aiken, South Carolina, is important, as being the most clear and intelligent statement, which I was able to obtain after considerable inquiry.

Report on the Communication of Syphilis through the medium of Vaccine Virus, amongst the inhabitants of Graniteville and vicinity—1866. By W. F. PERCIVAL, M. D., of Aiken, S. C.

AIKEN, Nov. 15th, 1866.

Professor JOSEPH JONES, M. D.,

DEAR SIR:

I received your letter yesterday, and enclose a copy of my report on Spurious vaccination, with pleasure. I intended sending it to one of the Medical journals, but have never had time to revise and prepare it for publication; the *facts*, however, are all stated.

I am with high esteem, yours very respectfully,

W. F. PERCIVAL.

Spurious Vaccination.—The Epidemiological Society of London, prepared four questions on the subject of vaccination, to be addressed to the most eminent Medical men in Europe. The third was as follows:

Have you any reason to believe, or suspect, that lymph from a true Jennerian vesicle, has ever been a vehicle for syphilitic or other constitutional infection? Among the number who responded, (over 400,) but three asserted their belief; twenty-seven in doubt, and nine had no experience. The rest asserted that it could not be done.

In a report from the College of the Faculty of Medicine, at Prague, the following language is used: "The possibility of inoculation with Syphilis by means of vaccination, (although not a single completely attested fact is known in this country,) is not to be excluded, for the conveyance of Syphilis, by means of inoculation, has been placed beyond a doubt."

In the face of so much testimony against the possibility of such an occurrence, the following report will perhaps throw some light on the subject.

About the last of April, 1866, I was requested to take charge of some cases of Spurious vaccination, at the manufacturing village of Graniteville. One hundred and fifty cases were presented for examination, men, women, and children, of all ages, from fifty years to twelve months. The larger proportion were operatives in the Factory, the others engaged in out-door work. There was every variety of constitution, from the pale and attenuated girl, to the hardy and robust laborer. Of the one hundred and fifty cases, ninety-three had been previously vaccinated. The appearance of the sore was identical in every case, viz: an excavated ulcer, of circular form, with raised and hardened edges and base. They varied in size, from one half to two inches in diameter, covered with grey or dark sloughy matter, and secreting unhealthy pus. There was no appearance of granulation. In some cases ulcers of a similar character, appeared on the arms affected; others on the opposite arm, and in a few on the lower limbs. In some, abscesses formed on the inside of the arm, and in nearly all the axillary glands were inflamed, and many suppurated. A thick and unhealthy crust would form, to be soon separated by the pus which accumulated beneath. In one case, there was a copper-colored eruption on the body and limbs; in two or three the hair dropped off. None of these cases were in the primary stage. The disease had existed from three to eight weeks. Most of them pursued their ordinary avocations, as far as possible, and complained of no constitutional symptoms, or any loss of appetite.

The history of these cases, as given to me by the individuals first vaccinated, was, that they had obtained the virus from a man whom they afterward discovered to have had primary Syphilis. One was vaccinated from another, and so it spread. None of the ulcers had evidenced any tendency to heal. One of the worst cases was a man who, two years previously, had small-pox.

The usual treatment, both constitutional and local, for venerial ulcers, effected a cure in from three to six weeks.

It might be supposed that the predisposing cause of the ulcers, existed in a vitiated condition of the blood, dependent on local causes, but I had twelve or fifteen cases in other localities, some of them ten miles distant; all of these had obtained the virus with which they were vaccinated at Graniteville. All of these were strong and healthy individuals. Again, most of the cases reported had been vaccinated a short time previously and had progressed in the usual manner without any trouble, showing that no local cause had produced any derangement of their system.

As I did not see the individual from whom the virus was first obtained, I am unable to say that he really had primary Syphilis.

I cannot therefore draw positive conclusions from the above cases, and only present the report as information.

On the other hand, many of the Confederate Surgeons, entertained views similar to those announced by Dr. Habersham, and denied that any of the cases of Spurious vaccination were syphilitic in their origin or relations.

Thus Dr. S. F. Stout, of Pulaski, Tennessee, formerly Medical Director of the General Hospitals attached to the Army of Tennessee, in his reply (dated near Pulaski, Nov. 19th, 1866,) to my inquiries, says:

I am not satisfied that there occurred a well authenticated instance of the propagation of secondary Syphilis by means of the so-called Spurious vaccine matter. I think that the injurious effects were chiefly produced upon persons already diseased syphilitic, scorbutic, or while living in an atmosphere infected by the causes of gangrene and erysipelas. A vast majority of these cases were those of individuals, who had been previously vaccinated, and in very many instances, the virus used was taken from the arms of re-vaccinated individuals. Thus common pus, and even ichor, was no doubt inoculated, which produced effects similar to those that are caused by a wound, received while dissecting a dead body, modified in many instances, no doubt, by the condition of the patient's health, and the morbific influences to which he was exposed.

Prior to my assumption of authority to take steps to stop the evil, I am satisfied that there were several errors in practice among our troops. First, the order requiring all soldiers to be vaccinated, whether they had been previously effectually vaccinated or not. This order was literally interpreted and acted on by the superintendents of vaccination appointed by the Surgeon General. Secondly, many soldiers ignorant of the characteristics of genuine vaccinia, vaccinated themselves, or each other. without consulting a Surgeon. Thus, no doubt, common pus, and even ichorus matter were often inserted. Thirdly, When variola first appeared in our army, so great was the fear of the disease, and the consequent anxiety to vaccinate everybody in the army, or in its vicinity, that the temptation to the Surgeon to use any virus within his reach, was very great. Thus much matter was used, which ought to have been rejected by Surgeons.

In my investigations I could not learn of a single well authenticated instance in which due care had been taken in the selection of the virus, whether in the form of lymph, or of the dried scab, that was accompanied by the evils of so-called Spurious vaccination, in a perfectly healthy individual, in an atmosphere uninfected by erysipelas or gangrene. Believing my conclusions to be correct, when as Medical Director of the hospitals I undertook to relieve the army of the evil, I made provisions to supply it with virus taken only from the arms of healthy children, who had *never before been effectually vaccinated.* By the zeal and energy of medical officers designated at every hospital post, from supplies of virus obtained from the Surgeon General, S. P. Moore, and Surgeon J. C. Mullins, superintendent of vaccination of my department, appointed by me, the army in the field and the hospitals in the rear were amply furnished with virus from healthy children. No soldier was vaccinated with matter taken from another soldier. The supply was so abundant, that there was not temptation to use any other part of the dried crust than the vitreous, mahogany-colored portion. I recommended, that no soldier who had been vaccinated within a few years past, and who had the characteristic mark, should be re-vaccinated, unless positively known to have been exposed to variolous contagion; and especially, if he were labouring under any form of Syphilis, was scorbutic, or was living in an atmosphere infected with gangrene or erysipelas.

Under this practice, the so-called *Spurious* vaccination disappeared from our army, and before the close of the war it might be said to have ceased to exist in Georgia.

Having thus far entered into a statement of the impressions I have, and of facts bearing upon the subject, it may not be amiss to say to you, that my observations and experience during the war has confirmed my faith in the prophylactic powers of the Jennerian virus. I use the term Jennerian to designate that vaccine virus, which has been propagated from that originally supplied by Jenner. The immunity of so many thousands of soldiers and officers witnessed during the war, and the comparatively small number of the vaccinated who were attacked with variola or varioloid, enhance my estimate of the protective power of vaccinia, rather than diminishes it, as has been the case with many, whose field of observation has been comparatively smaller than mine.

I have no data, by which to form an opinion, as to the relative frequency and nature of the foul gangrenous ulcers attendant upon vaccination in the United States forces. In the Second Section of the present inquiry, we have quoted the testimony of Dr. Hamilton to show that they were to a great extent, as in the

Confederate Army, referable to the depressed and scorbutic condition of the soldiers.

Dr. Wooward, in Circular No. 6, War Department, Surgeon-General's Office, p. 127, affirms that the accidents attendant upon vaccination in the United States Army, were generally regarded by the Medical officers, as "the expression of scorbutic or other cachectic conditions of the patients, and not due to any poisonous admixture with the vaccine virus; and it was frequently observed that the same scab which had produced a number of successful vaccinations, would; in other men vaccinated at the same time, produce the ulcers referred to."

It appears, however, that some of the United States Medical officers, held that a portion at least of these abnormal affections following vaccination, were due to the admixture with the syphilitic poison, as will be seen by the following extracts from an article on Spurious Vaccination, by Geo. H. Hubbard, M.D., late Brevet Lieut.-Col., and Surgeon U. S. Vols., published in the Philadelphia Medical and Surgical Reporter, February 10, 1866, p. 103.

On the last day of November, 1863, I reached Fort Smith, Arkansas, under an assignment to duty as Medical Director of the Army of the Frontier.

My attention was immediately called to several hundred men disabled in consequence of spurious vaccination, and a board of medical officers was soon after organized, by command of Major General Schofield, to investigate its origin, etc.

This Board made a detailed report, from which, from reports of other medical officers, and from personal observation, I was enabled to arrive at the following facts and conclusions.

It was definitely ascertained that the virus which caused all these cases came from persons who had been vaccinated in the rebel army, or by rebel Surgeons.

This virus was used by ignorant medical officers and by self-inoculation among the men, till more than five hundred were infected.

The Board reported that—"Soon after the operation was performed. the points at which the matter was inserted commenced to itch and inflame, and by the second or third day, pustules were formed, of a yellowish color, which rapidly increased in size, and in a few days burst. In some a scab formed, but in all, open ulcers were formed by the tenth day, and which furnished a thin ichorous discharge.

"At the time we examined the patients, some had well marked Hunterian chancre; some had large excavated ulcers, with edges elevated above the raw and surrounding induration; the centres, when not recently cauterized, were of a brownish hue—some, whose primary ulcers were about healed, had secondary symptoms, such as swelling and ulceration of the glands in different parts of the body; while others had pain and stiffening of the joints.

"The disease was brought to the 1st Arkansas Infantry by deserters from the Confederate army, and in our opinion it is Syphilis."

The following is from my official report to the Surgeon General:—" I have no reason to believe that in any one case did this virus produce a true vaccine pustule, or had any of the protecting power of vaccination.

" The ulcers all possessed, in a greater or less degree, the well established pecu, liarites of veneral chancre, being of a specific and progressive nature, spreading in some cases to the size of a dollar, but usually about half that size; commonly round in shape, but often irregular, and usually of the depth of the true skin.

" All had ragged, elevated, indurated, and overhanging edges, little sensitive to the touch or even to caustics; while the bottom of the ulcer, (especially under these indurated edges,) was excessively sensitive.

" All discharged dark ill-conditioned pus, which in many cases caused painful excoriation of the surrounding skin, and when transferred to other parts of the body, reproduced ulcers like the original; in this way, chancres were produced on the penis in several cases.

" Cases precisely similar occurred in the Indian Brigade, stationed at Fort Gibson in the Cherokee nation.

" Acting Assistant Surgeon Miller, on duty at that post, reported as follows:

" Besides the cases occurring among the troops, it has spread among the people to an alarming extent by self-inoculation.

" In a large proportion of the cases, consecutive symptoms have appeared; suppuration of the lymphatic glands in the axilla, sore throat, exanthematous eruptions, etc.

"The cases occurring among the troops have received the ordinary treatment for Syphilis, and in most cases with excellent results.

" The mischief was wide spread before the true character of the disease was recognized, so that few cases have had prompt abortive treatment, and many are, in consequence, permanently disabled.

"Nearly every case has required constitutional treatment, in addition to local treatment of the chancre.

" The milder caustic applications proving insufficient, in many cases, acid nitrate of mercury was used to clear away the indurated edges, when the ulcer usually healed rapidly under mildly stimulating applications."

" Six cases of well marked small-pox occurred in men who had previously suffered severely from this venereal inoculation.—*Med. and Surg. Reporter,*—Feby. 19th, 1866,—p. 103.

Up to the commencement of the recent civil war, the belief was almost universal that secondary syphilis could not thus be communicated by vaccination.

In the Papers relating to the History and Practice of Vaccination, contained in the Report of the General Board of Health, presented to both Houses of Parliament, by command of Her Majesty—London, 1857—Mr. Simon called for the opinion of the profession at home and abroad on the general question.

"Have you any reason to believe or suspect (a) that lymph from a true Jennerian vesicle has ever been a vehicle of syphilitic, scrofulous or other constitutional infection to the vaccinated person; (b) or that unintentional inoculation with some other disease, instead of the proposed vaccination, has occurred in the hands of a duly educated medical practitioner?"

In answer to this question a writer in the British and Foreign Medico-Chirurgical Review (October, 1857, Review iii., Small-pox and Vaccination), quotes the opinions of Hebra, which may be taken as expressing in a logical and lucid manner, the belief of the majority of the medical profession at that time.

"This widely-grasping question (says Hebra) requires several separate answers, because queries are made,—

"1. *Whether the lymph of a vaccine vesicle may, besides its peculiar virus, contain another infectious principle—e. g., that of syphilis?*

"2. *Whether constitutional non-infecting diseases, as, for instance, scrofula, may be transmitted by the inoculation of cow-pox matter?*

"3. *Whether a vaccine vesicle possesses such characters that it may easily be distinguished from other similar vesicles, blebs or pustules?*

"(I.) The transmissible infectious principles which have hitherto been recognized, by means of inoculation, are, the syphilitic virus contained in the pus of a chancre; and the virus contained in the cow-pox vesicle, and the small-pox pustule. The question, therefore, simply is, whether these morbid poisons have ever been mixed? Whether inoculation has ever taken place with such a mixture? And what results were obtained by such an operation? It is well known that compendious answers have, for some time past, been offered to these questions, chiefly the result of Sigmund's experiments. These answers agree in the following respects:

"Inoculation with secretions of this kind—viz., containing, as it were, several special poisons, either produced no effect at all, or only generated a chancre, by inoculating a mixture of pus from the chancre and vaccine lymph; and only cow-pox, by inoculating a combination of vaccine lymph and blenorrhagic matter. Hence one morbid state only was produced, either cow-pox or syphilis; the latter circumstance being a proof that both poisons are not *simultaneously transmissible*. This opinion is supported by the experience of Heim, Ricord, Bousquet, Taupin. Landouzy, Friedenger, &c.

"(II). It is maintained in many quarters that the blood of persons suffering from secondary syphilis may serve as a vehicle to the infectious principle; but were even this theory found correct, it would have no prejudicial effect on the practice of vaccination, because we know from experiments made for the purpose (Heim), and from accidental inoculation, that regardless of the quality of vaccine lymph, the latter may be inoculated from syphilitic upon sound individuals; and, on the other hand, from sound subjects upon such as are under the influence of systemic syphilis, without propagating syphilis along with the cow-pox.

"What has here been proved of syphilis, must *á fortiori*, hold good as regards other constitutional morbid states, as direct inoculations with the secretions peculiar to these diseases have always yielded a negative result.

"But although it is abundantly proved that scrofula, tubercular affections, rickets, cancer, and other blood diseases cannot be transmitted by means of their own secretions, or along with the vaccine lymph, we should nevertheless, if possible, avoid vaccinating diseased persons, because experience has taught us, as regards adults and children, that the phenomena of vaccination may awake—i. e., render worse—dormant affections, and that moreover, the cow-pox vesicle easily degenerates upon such individuals. These latter vesicles are nevertheless adapted for further propagation even when they take an imperfect development, because a positive result, a regular development of the vesicle, and sufficient protection against small-pox have been observed in cases where vaccine lymph was transferred from weakly, scrofulous, and rickety subjects upon perfectly sound individuals.

"(III.) Every morbid appearance on the cutaneous envelope has its own peculiar characters, by which it may be distinguished from all other similar phenomena; the vaccine vesicle presents, in the like manner, sufficiently striking peculiarities as to form, size, number, locality, and peculiarity as regards its course, to enable the observer easily to establish a distinction between the same ánd other vesicular, bullar or pustular eruptions."

We shall examine these doctrines and conclude these *Researches on Spurious Vaccination*, with an examination of the following questions :

(1st.) *The possibility of communicating Tuberculosis and Cancer by Inoculation.*

(2d.) *The possibility of communicating Secondary or Constitutional Syphilis by Inoculation.*

(3d.) *The possibility of communicating the poison of Syphilis through the medium of the Vaccine Virus.*

I. True Tubercle is organized ; that is, it is composed of living cells, and during its growth it resembles, to a certain extent, fresh granulations. These soft fragile cells and nuclei, resembling the gland cells of the lymphatic glands, are to be regarded as the characteristic living element of tubercle. According to this view, Tubercle resembles malignant growths.

M. Villemin's researches appear to have settled the question of the inoculability of Tubercle. This observer affirms that he had succeeded in reproducing tubercle by inoculation, again and again, in rabbits, not only when taken from the human subject, but also when derived from the cow ; and farther, that the tubercular matter thus produced in one rabbit, could be in like manner transmitted to another. (*Gazette Hebdomadaire*, 1866).

Dr. Lebert, Professor at Breslau, has succeeded in introducing tubercle into the system by subcutaneous injection, and thus confirmed M. Villemin's experiments. Dr. Lebert's experiments were made with Guinea pigs and rabbits, and both grey and yellow tuberculous matter were employed, as well as liquid from a cavity : the nape of the neck was the spot chosen for injection, and the amount introduced varied from fifty centigrammes to a gramme, diluted and triturated with distilled water. The result of his experiments was the finding of tubercles not only in the lungs, but in other organs, as the liver, spleen, plurae and pericardium. In some experiments, the tubercles were found in large portions of the lymphatic system. Microscopic examination revealed the identity of the tubercles thus formed in animals by inoculation, with those of man.

Tubercle still farther resembles malignant growths, in that the original growth causes the formation of new tubercles in its neighborhood and thus gradually infects large tracts of living and previously healthy tissue. It is possible in many cases, by carefully comparing the symptoms during life, with the results of post-mortem examination, to trace the gradual propagation, of tubercle from a well defined centre.

It is not my design to discuss, at this time, the cause and mode of origin of tubercle, or its relations to inflammation, and to defective nutrition ; my design has been simply to show that there are facts and experiments proving the possibility of transmitting. the disease from one animal to another by inoculation. And whilst we are unacquainted with a single fact which illustrates in any manner the relations of vaccination to tuberculosis, at the same time it must be admitted that we need farther experiments and light upon this subject : and we know just enough to create a prejudice against the indiscriminate use of vaccine matter from scrofulous and tuberculous subjects. Dr. George

Budd, of London, in his valuable work on Diseases of the Liver, has recorded a large number of facts to show, not only that cancer may be disseminated by *inoculation*, or by the mere contact of a sound part with a part affected with cancer, without any direct vascular connexion between them ; and by cancerous matter conveyed by lymphatics and veins to other parts of the body : but that cancer may even be propagated by inoculation, or by injection of cancerous matter into veins, from one animal to another.

The facts recorded by Dr. Budd, illustrate in the clearest manner the first two modes of the dissemination of cancer, in the human being ; and to support the third proposition he cites the following experiments :

Professor Langenbeck, injected into the veins of a dog some pulp taken from a cancer which had just been removed from a living body. At the end of some weeks the dog began to waste rapidly. It was then killed, and several cancerous tumors were found in its lungs.

Another instance to the same effect, taken from a German periodical, is related in the Provincial Medical Journal for september-tember 23, 1843. Some cells were collected from a black liquid in the orbit of a mare affected with melanosis, and were inoculated into the conjunctiva and lachrymal gland of an old horse. These merely caused a black spot on the conjunctiva, which extended very slowly ; but about the sixteenth week after inoculation, melanosis of the lachrymal gland was very decided ; it had invaded the whole organ, and pushed the globe of the eye forward. Some of the melanotic matter, taken from the same mare, was injected into the veins of the neck of a dog, who died suddenly whilst hunting, three weeks after the operation. There was found in the left lung a melanotic tumor, which was ruptured, and which contained a brown, coffee-colored fluid, abounding in cells.

So many instances have occurred of cancer of the penis in men whose wives had cancer of the womb, that many physicians have been led to believe that the disease in these instances was propagated by contagion. (On the Diseases of the Liver by George

Budd, M.D., Third Edition, London, 1857, chapter iv., pp. 388-416).

It would in like manner, be foreign to our purpose to enter into any speculations as to the cause of cancer, or into an examination of the question, whether the germ of the disease be a true parasite, introduced from without; or whether cancer is generated within the body, or of the materials of the body, under the influences of certain agencies.

We will have accomplished our purpose in recording these facts, if we succeed in directing the attention of the profession in this country, to the necessity of greater attention to the condition of the subjects selected for the propagation of the vaccine disease.

We proceed now to the consideration of the second and more important question, which relates to the propagation of one of the most destructive poisons in its action upon the human race.

II. The formal and persevering denial by eminent surgeons, that Secondary Syphilitic disease could be communicated by contact, and the adoption of this theory by a large and influential school, has inflicted much domestic misery and led to most unwarrantable and destructive carelessness in the process of vaccination.

The question of the commincation, by contact and inoculation of Secondary Syphilis, is of vast importance in its bearing upon the human race, and should not be settled dogmatically—in fact it is not in any manner a question of belief, but of facts.

As early as 1498, Gaspard Torella affirmed that he had often seen the unweaned child infected by the sore breasts of its mother, and then bestow upon its nurse, who fondled and kissed it, the same unfortunate endowments.

Many of the older writers appear to have entertained no doubt with reference to the possibility of communicating constitutional syphilis. The following testimony is from William Clowes, who wrote more than two centuries and a half ago:

> I have also knowne divers persons infected, who have had in all other parts of the bodie manifest signes thereof, as dolors, tumors, ulcers, and venemous pustules, &c. And yet in the parts aforesaid, no paine, or any signe thereof: so that their opinion is not to be observed, which affirme, that this disease is ingendred onely, by the com-

pany of uncleane persons: for I have knowne not many yeares past, three good and honest Midwives infected with this disease, called *Lues Venerea*, by bringing abed three infected women, of three infected children, which infection was chiefly fixed upon the Midwives fingers and hands, &c. What should I speake of young sucking children, whereof divers have beene grievously vexed with this disease, and some of them a moneth, two, three or foure moneths old, and some of them a yeare old, some foure or five yeares old, and some of them sixe or seaven yeares old, amongst, which sort, I thought it good here to note a certaine wench, the daughter of one *Sare*, of twelve yeares of age, the which I cured, in the yeare of oure Lord 1567, who was greatly infected with this sicknesse in many parts of her body, having thereon painfull nodes or hard swellings and ulcers, with corruption of the bones, and yet no signe in the most suspected parts, neither by reason of debilitie was able to have committed any such act, but it is not to be doubted, but that she received the infection, either from the parents, the which cure of some is supposed uncertaine, whether, children begotten by infected parents, may bee cured or not: or else she was infected, as divers are, by sucking the corrupt milke of some infected nurse, of whom I have cured many, for such milke is engendred of infected bloud, and I may not here in conscience overpasse, to forewarne thee good Reader, of such lewde and filthie nurses: for that in the yeare 1583, it chanced that three young children, all borne in this citie of London, all of one parish, or very neere together, and being of honest parentage, were put to nurse, the one in the countrie, and the other two were nursed in this citie of London: but within lesse than halfe a yeare, they were all three brought home to their parents and friends, grievously infected with this great and odious disease, by their wicked and filthy nurses: Then their parents seeing them thus miserably spoiled and consumed by extreme paines, and great breaking out upon their bodies, and being so young, sick and weake, unpossible to be weaned, were forced, as nature doth binde, to seeke by all meanes possible to preserve these poore silly infants, which else had died most pitifully. To be briefe, ere ever those children could be cured, they had infected five sundry good and honest nurses: I cured one of the children, and the nurse which gave it sucke, the other two children and their nurses were also cured by others, but one of the children lived not long after, as I was given to understand. Also friendly Reader, I read of late in a certain history, written by *Ambrose Pare*, in his 2. book, intreating of the causes of *Lues Venerea*, which history indeed is worthy the rehearsal!: "An honest Citizen saith he, granted his most chaste wife, that she should nurse the childe which she was lately delivered of, if she would keepe a nurse to be partaker of the travell and paines: the nurse that she tooke by chance, was infected with *Lues Venerea*, therefore she did presently infect the foster childe, and he the mother, and she the husband, and he two children which he had daily at his table and bed, not knowing of that poison which he did nourish in his own body and intrals. But when the mother considered and perceived, that her childe did not prosper or profit by the nourishment, but continually cried and waxed wayward, desired me to tell her the cause of that disease, neither was it any hard matter to doe, for his body was full of the small-pocks, whelkes, and venerous pustules: and the brests of the nurses and mother being looked on, were eroded with virulent ulcers: and the body of the father and his two sonnes, the one about three yeares, and the other foure yeares of age, were infected with the like pustules and swellings that the childe had: therefore I shewed them that they were all infected with *Lues Venerea*, whose beginnings, and as it were provocations, were spred abroad by the nurse that was hired, by her maligne infection. I cured them all, and by the helpe of God, brought them to health, except the sucking childe, which died in the cure: and the nurse being called before the magistrates, was punished in prison and whipped closely, and had been publikely whipped through all the streets of the citie, if it had not been for the honors of that unfortunate family." Thus we see children infected by filthy nurses, and sometimes nurses be infected by giving sucke to such infected children. And now to returne to my former purpose, the disease, as saith *Nicholas Masa*, whose counsell and direction in the cure of this disease I have greatly observed. The disease because it hath a flowing matter, being once entred into any part of the body, proceedeth on from part to part, never resting until it hath corrupted the liver, with the ill disposition of this infection especially. When it toucheth any such part, as hath in it an apt disposition to admit such infection, as when the action or force of the agent is wrought and imprinted in the patient, fitly affected to receive the same forme, and so it disperseth itselfe through the whole bodie: likewise this sickness is many times bred in the mouth, by eating and drinking with infected persons, and sometimes onely by breathings: and *Almanor* a learned Physition setteth downe for truth, that this disease may be taken by kissing, and sometimes by lying in the bed with them, or by lying in the sheets after them: also it is said to come by sitting on the same stoole of easement, where some infected person frequenteth, and sometimes such as have been cured of this disease, fall into it againe by wearing their old infected apparell: all which causes of this disease I rather set downe, for that I would thereby admonish as many, as shall read this treatise, to be carefull of themselves in this behalfe, and to shun as much as may be, all such occasions.—*A Profitable and Necessarie Booke of Observations for all those that are burned with the flame of Gun-powder, &c.: By William Clowes. London; M. Dawson, 1637. pp. 151-2-3.*

Gideon Harvey, in his "Venus Unmasked," published two hundred years ago, expresses similar views:

4. *Probl.* How many various ways doth the Pox exert its Contagion? No external part is impowered to transmit its infection immediately, except where its suscepted: so we observe the Venereal parts to be infectory immediately upon the susception of virulency, but not through kissing, sucking of the breast, by sweat, or through any other parts but themselves. So the mouth that's infected by kissing, or sucking a thorow pockified whore's tet, is capable of immediately infecting anothers lips by kissing, or any other part by sucking it, because the pocky Miasms are neer; but not by copulation, or sweat, &c., because the contagion cannot be crept so far. Experience verifies this dictate. Is it not an ordinary trick of Wenchers (as *Musa* relates) to suck whores tongues, and tets of their breast and yet those, whom they know have been pockified many years about their lower parts, and for that reason though their appetites are furious, yet dare not be dabbling, but the other they reiterate a thousand times over without the least hazzard? An instance for the other part of the dictate, which I had from my

my first master in Physick, that wonder of Physicians Prof. *Job. Antonid. vander Linden. p. m.* the profoundest Commentator on *Hippocrates* and *Celsus*, that ever any age presented, whom I heard that most famous *Professor Regius Guido Patin* intitulate the *Dutch Hippocrates*. He during his luculent practice at *Amsterdam*, had a Merchants Prentice in cure of an Gonorrhe, and a blistered, or cankered like mouth; both symptoms he confest to have started upon him at the same time. The excellent Professor being curious and admiring at the rarity of such distant symptoms emerging at once, extorted an ingenuous confession from his Patient, upon pretence that it would facilitate and abreviate the cure: the other without any longer suspense impudently told him, his tongue was as unfortunate as his tayl; a sort of Diabolick fatyrism, outvying *Arctius flagello de Principi*, and very like a *Dutch* invention. What insued? this bastard at a *Besoeck* (an invitation thats usually made to young folks, preliminary to all Weddings) accosted himself to two pretty Damsels, and being planted between them, oft flanckt to the right, and in a kiss pledged his right hand man, and so to the left, and performed the like duty there. But the tragick event may imprint a dread upon all young women. A short time after their lips felt hot, inflamed, grew sore and ulcered, one named it the thrush, another a sore mouth vulgar applications rather promoted than checkt the evil, wherein they persisted so long that accessory accidents, as sordid ulcers of the palat and tonsils, nocturnal pains, &c. moved a jealousie of the fowl disease. Here you may remark, how innocently the poor lasses pessundated their fortunes. The reflexion of this relation upon the latter part of the dictate I commit to your own thoughts.

2. A Wench or Monsieur by that time they are thorow pockified, are infectious in any part where ever the Pox bursts out, because the virulent seminaries are propagated quite through the body, which exhaling at the places affected, transport the contagion. What the *thorow-pox* is expect below; so that when the malady is tumefyed to so high a flood, its time for Nurses, Physicians, and all visiters to stand off: upon such occasions a person may be infected by drinking out of the same vessel (provided the spittle adhering be warm still,) as we have heard of many; (*Leonardus Botallus* adduceth an observation of a patient of his, of a chast and religious converse, who was stigmatized by a peculiar pledging of his familiar, then under a sore affliction of a *thorow-pox*. His lips inflamed, afterwards ulcered, his jaw bone grew carious, and was miserably rackt with nocturnal arthritick pains.) By trying of a warm Pocky Glove; by succeeding a virulent Patient on a close stool; by shifting of him, or making his bed whilest the sheets continue warm; as *Nicol. Massa's* friend and Patient, who incurred this evil, by touching the sheets, one lay in, that was lame of a *Neapolitan* ulcer in his legg; and that old woman in *Horst's observ.* aged fifty-six, tending a Pocky fellow in his lying in, was seized of the same disease in as furious a degree as her Master: and by kissing, witness *Faventinus*, who knew a young man, that contracted this evil by oft kissing a fowl slut. The initial symptoms appeared about his mouth; his privities, which otherwise might have bin suspected, appearing free from all contagion. To this I'l parallel another; one Mrs. &c. then a pocky inhabitant of the *Hague*, having run the gantlop of several cures, Hydrotick and Mercurial, at last proved with child; her reckoning being expired, she was brought to bed of a Monster, in all particulars resembling a living child; saving the skin, which was abominally ciphered with spots and

botches. This object of *mercy upon us* was committed to the care of a Nurse, the Infant aspiring to higher things, bad the world adieu. But the unhappy Nurse had cause to curse her late Foster-child, her breasts and head ulcered, a *Caries* got into the *cranium*, the Pox took possession of the poor woman's carcase, for want of a purse to release her. The pocky original Mistris &c. was proclaimed barbarous by a whole Jury of Matrons, for refusing relief to the disastered woman. In all these transactions the *Pater Familias* stood it out vigorously with a fresh countenance, no sign contradicting his pancratick health. Just such another mischance *Musa Brasavolus*, tells us, befell a nurse that suckled one Sr. *Urobo's* child, thorowly conspurcated with the Pox. The observation hereupon infers this a *thorow-pox*, and consequently must prove infectious in all parts of the body. Physicians in this case run a great risk in feeling pulses, and approaching such Patients in their sweats.—*Venus Unmasked, or a More Exact Discovery of the Venereal Evil, or French Disease: By Gideon Harvey, London; T. Grismond*, 1665. *pp.* 94-5-6-7-8-9.

In like manner Daniel Turner in his work on Syphilis, published in 1717, maintains the contagious nature of constitutional Syphilis:

And this I intend shall suffice for its *Chronology* or Time, the *Topology* or Place, and the *Histriography* or Account of the Disease in general; which, with some other Writers thereon, we shall now define, *A venomous or contagious Distemper, for the most part contracted by impure Coition, at least some Con.rc! cf the Genitals cf both Sexes, or some other lewed and filthy Dalliance between each other that way tending.*

I said *for the most part*, because it is beyond Controversy, the Infection is also communicated by other ways, as from Pocky Parents by Inheritance; by sucking an infected Nurse, to the Child; suckling a diseased Child, to the Nurse; lying also in Bed with the Diseased, without any Carnal Familiarity; by which, though it may be possible for strong and vigorous Bodies to escape, yet are the tender ones, especially of little Infants, very likely to be contaminated, as I have more Reason to believe than by bare Imagination.

There are several other more uncommon Ways of giving as well as receiving the *Venereal* Venom; some of which I have already imparted to the World in short Remarks upon a Quack Libel, Printed several Years past: But the Thought of such vile Monsters, and their execrable Practices, is too shocking (unless to the Dregs of humane Nature) to bear even a Repetition of Circumstances, and fit only for a detestable *Gonologium* or Collection of Smutt and Obscenity, in which I am told, they have been inserted, as some of the Author's own Observations.

As for those fancied Ways of catching it by common Conversation, drinking after one, sitting on the same Close-stool, drawing on a Glove, wiping on the Napkin or Towel, after the infected Person, with a hundred the like Stories; I believe in our time (whatever may have happened formerly) there is no great Danger: Yet we find in one of our late Chronicles, that these and such like Imaginations, were so strongly rivetted in Men's Minds at that time, even those of the better and more learned sort, that it was one of the Articles against a noted Cardinal, That he had breathed on the King, when he, the said Cardinal, had this Disease upon him

Which you will find in *Baker's* Chronicle, and of which Passage Dr. *Harvey* has also taken Notice. *Hildanus* likewise tells us of a young Gentlewoman, who contracted the same, by only putting on the Apparel of a Gentleman (that it seems was pox'd) at a Masquerade, of which, through Modesty concealing her Illness (which first of all had seized the *Pudenda*) till she was past Recovery, she deceased. The good Man's Credulity, at least his Charity, might however be abus'd in this Relation, as the young Lady perhaps was also after the Masque, otherwise than by simply putting on the Habit. But were it so as the Case is stated, there is nothing therein much more admirable than what the same great Man recites of a whole Family he knew infected, viz. the Wife with three Children and a fourth in the Womb, as also a Maid Servant, by the Husband, who had got the Distemper in their Absence only by sleeping in the same bed with his Man Servant, whom he after understood was broke out with this Distemper.

The Relation of *Horst.* and *Hornung.* are yet more strange, of several People infected in the Bagnio, by having the same Scarificator apply'd after Cupping, as had been used to a *Venereal* Patient: Which seems a like credible with that of the Priest poxed at his Ear, in the time of confessing a wanton Nun; the venomous Breath from her Mouth defiling the holy Father: But enough of this.—*Syphilis; a Practical Dissertation on the Venereal Disease: By Daniel Turner, London; R. Bonwicke & Co.*, 1717. *pp.* 10-11-12.

John Hunter, in his Treatise on the Venereal Disease, gives a number of instances of the communication of secondary Syphilis, from which we select the following:

A lady was delivered of a child on the 30th of September, 1776. The infant being weakly, and the quantity of milk in the mother's breasts abundant, it was judged proper to procure the child of a person in the neighborhood to assist in keeping the breasts in a proper state. It is worthy of remark that the lady kept her own child to the right breast, the stranger to the left, In about six weeks the nipple of the left breast began to inflame, and the glands of the axilla to swell. A few days after several small ulcers were formed about the nipple, which, spreading rapidly, soon communicated and became one ulcer, and at last the whole nipple was destroyed. The tumor in the axilla subsided, and the ulcer in the breast healed in about three months from its first appearance. On inquiry, about this time, the child of the stranger was found to be short-breathed, had the thrush, and died tabid, with many sores on different parts of the body. The patient now complained of shooting pains in different parts of the body, which were succeeded by an eruption on the arms, legs, and thigh, many of which became ulcers.

She was now put under a mercurial course, with a decoction of sarsaparilla. Mercury was tried in a variety of forms: in solution, in pills internally, and externally in the form of ointment. It could not be continued above a few days at a time, as it always brought on fever or purging, with extreme pain in the bowels. In this state she remained till March 16th, 1779, when she was delivered of another child in a diseased state. The child was committed to the care of a wet nurse, and lived about nine weeks; the cuticle peeling off in various parts, and a scabby eruption covering the whole body. The child died.

Soon after the death of the child, the nurse complained of headache and sore throat, together with ulceration of the breasts. Various remedies were given to her, but she determined to go into a public hospital, where she was salivated, and after some months she was discharged, but not cured of the disease. The bones of the nose and palate exfoliated, and in a few months she also died tabid.

Of the various remedies tried by the lady herself, none succeeded so well as sea-bathing. About the end of May she began a course of the Lisbon diet-drink, and continued it with regularity about a month, dressing the sores with laudanum, by which treatment the sores healed up; and in September she was delivered of another child, free from external marks of disease, but very sickly; and it died in the course of the month.

About a twelve month after, the sores broke out again, and, although mercurial dressings and internal medicines were given, remained for a twelve month, when they began again to heal up. * * * * * * *

The third case was of a gentleman, where the transplanted tooth remained, without giving the least disturbance, for about a month, when the edge of the gum began to ulcerate, and the ulceration went on until the tooth dropped out. Some time after, spots appeared almost everywhere on the skin; they had not the truly venereal appearance, but were redder or more transparent, and more circumscribed He had also a tendency to a hectic fever, such as restlessness, want of sleep, loss of appetite, and headache. After trying several things, and not finding relief, he was put under a course of mercury, and all disease disappeared according to the common course of the cure of the venereal disease, and we thought him well; but some time after the same appearances returned, with the addition of swelling in the bones of the metacarpus. He was now put under another course of mercury, more severe than the former, and in the usual time, all the symptoms again disappeared. Several months after the same eruption came out again, but not in so great a degree as before, and without any other attendant symptoms. He a third time took mercury, but it was only ten grains of corrosive sublimate in the whole, and he got quite wel', The time between his first taking mercury and his being cured was a space of three years.—*The Works of John Hunter, with Notes, edited by James F. Palmer. Vol. ii., p 475, 476; p. 484.*

In an extract from a letter to Dr. Duncan, published in the "*Medical Commentaries for the years* 1783–84–85" it is said that a new disease has lately been discovered in London, occasioned by the transplanting of teeth from the head of one person to that of another. The mortality from it is computed at nearly two deaths to ten diseases ; and about one in every hundred, who receive teeth by transplantation, are affected with the disease. Ulcerations of the throat and gums, and eruptions on the skin, are the chief marks of the disease. When death takes place it is from the occurrence of sphacelus. For five or six weeks after

transplanting, the teeth look well, and are as firm as the others."
pp. 490, 491.

In the third volume of the London Medical Transactions, Dr. William Watson, Vice President of the Royal Society, recorded an interesting case, illustrating the terrible effects of transplanting teeth, from which we extract the following particulars:

An unmarried lady, in the twenty-first year of her age, of a delicate habit, but in other respects in perfect health, observing one of the incisors of her upper jaw to become black and carious, determined on having it replaced by a sound tooth. This was accordingly done by an able dentist; the tooth which was introduced, being taken from the mouth of a person apparently healthy in every particular. At the end of a month, her mouth, which had continued all that time a little tender, became very painful. Her upper gums were at first inflamed and enlarged; afterwards they were discolored and ulcerated. This ulceration spread very fast, insomuch that the gums of the upper jaw were corroded away, and the alveoli left bare. Before another month was at an end, the ulceration occupied the whole space under the upper lip between the teeth and the nose; it extended likewise to the cheeks and throat, which were corroded by large, deep and fetid ulcers. Soon after this, part of the alveoli of the upper jaw became carious, one of her teeth dropped out; and in a few days a second tooth, together with the transplanted tooth, which hitherto had remained firm in its place. About this time blotches appeared on her face, neck and various parts of her body; and several of these became ulcerated sores. The fetid discharges from her mouth and throat had for a considerable time deprived her of sleep; and the soreness of the parts had prevented her from taking nourishment. And, in addition to these, the soreness from the external ulcers induced such a degree of fever that her death was soon expected.

When Dr. Watson was consulted, concluding that all her fluids were in a most putrid and acrimonious state, he directed Peruvian bark combined with gum-myrrh in large doses. No benefit resulted from this plan, and the patient was placed upon alterative doses of mercury. The improvement was marked, the ulceration was arrested and the blotches began to disappear. The internal administration of mercury was abandoned, on account of its irritant effect upon the bowels, and the impression was kept up by rubbing mercurial ointment into her legs and thighs; this practice in like manner was attended with beneficial effects. In about ten or twelve days, the blotches had entirely disappeared and the ulcers of the mouth almost completely healed. The griping and purging, however, returned with such violence that Dr. Watson was compelled to abandon the mercury altogether. Small portions of the carious alveoli continued to exfoliate, the ulceration began again to spread, the patient labored under great weakness, with frequent returns of feverish heat, and was every night oppressed with colliquative sweats. Her strength gradually lessened, till death put an end to her sufferings.

As the progress of the disease was not impeded by the most powerful antiseptics in liberal doses, and as it gave way to mercurials even in small doses, there appeared to be good ground for believing that the taint was truly venereal: but Dr. Watson, although aware of the great subtilty of the venereal poison, was perplexed by the statement that the person from whom the tooth was taken was perfectly well, and never had any venereal taint.

Mr. Clement Hamerton, Surgeon to the Castletown Dispensary, has recorded in the Dublin Journal (March, 1841) cases illustrating the Introduction of Syphilis into the System, through other Channels than Sexual Intercourse, from which he draws the following conclusions:

A healthy child is applied to the breast of a venereal nurse; in a couple of weeks syphilis shows itself in the child. A venereal child is applied to the breast of a healthy woman; soon afterwards she gets a syphilitic sore of the breast, which contaminates her system. A servant girl sucks a venereal sore breast, she gets a venereal ulcer of the mouth, which taints her system. The midwife has a slight scratch on the palm of the hand, and in delivering a putrid venereal child, she gets a sore on the hand which infects her system; and lastly the husband of the midwife is diseased at the time the ulcer exists upon his wife's hand.

Dr. Egan has recorded (Dublin Quarterly Journal, May, 1846) several cases illustrating the contagiousness of Secondary Syphilis. In the first case the child was born apparently healthy; eight weeks afterwards syphilis appeared. An ulcer then presented itself upon the breast of the nurse, and Secondary Syphilis occurred. In the second case the child was born apparently healthy; about ten weeks afterwards a suspicious rash appeared, succeeded by blisters and fissures about the mouth; ulcers occurred on the nurse's breasts, and then a scaly eruption, and other secondary symptoms. Both cases were cured by anti-syphilitics. In the third case, the woman was a dry nurse, being disqualified by age from suckling. The child was unhealthy, and affected with sores, of a brownish color, about the nates and mouth, and a constant flow of saliva. A scratch appeared on the neck of the nurse, whether produced by a pin or torn by the nails of the child was uncertain; but being in the habit of bringing the child's mouth in contact with the affected part, in order to induce sleep, the disease was believed to be communicated through the abrasion, and the local effect was succeeded by an eruption, cured by anti-syphilitics.

In a trial which took place at Cork, Dr. O'Connor and Dr. Bull, gave evidence to show that a child affected with syphilitic eruption may convey the contagion to the nurse. (Lancet, July 4, 1846.)

Dr. Hector Gavin has given the history of a case, where a man and his wife, purporting never to have had syphilis, had a first child born perfectly free from any traces of the disease, subsequently to which the diseased child of a woman known to have had syphilis, but *supposed* to be cured, was placed to the wife's breast, the nipple being "cracked" at the time, and the disease was communicated.—(Lancet, July 18, 1846—Rankin's Abstract.)

Mr. Price of Margate has recorded the case of a woman who had syyhilis, which commenced in the nipple, from nursing an infected child. She gave birth to one child affected with the disease, and to another dead child. The child from whom this woman derived the disease had a very sore mouth and smelt very badly, and its father was known to have secondary syphilis of an aggravated character. Another respectable married woman, six weeks afterwards applied to Mr. Price, having syphilis, with a large sore on one of the nipples, and it turned out that this woman was nursing the same child which had affected the former nurse. This woman's own child also had the disease. This woman affected her husband. Two years and five months subsequently she gave birth to another child; this was affected with syphilis; twelve months subsequently another child was born similarly affected, and after this the mother was cured with iodide of potassium. Several very remarkable cases by Lallemand, Dr. King, and Dr. Mænick, will also be found in the twelfth volumn of the Medical Times—pp. 81, 176, 422—Rankin's Abstract, Vol. 10, p. 336.

According to M. Rizzi, who had an ample field for recording facts relating to congenital syphilis, in a large hospital under his charge in the city of Milan, if a woman contracts specific ulcerations on the breast by suckling an infected infant, mucous tubucles very frequently develop themselves on the vulva and about the anus; and the syphilis, although secondary, is transmissible by contact, so that a perfectly innocent woman may communicate the disease to her husband; and it behooves the medical attendant to be well apprised of this fact, as upon his knowledge of it, not only the health, but the peace of mind and honor of the individuals must rest.

Of 100 individuals with chancres on the breast from impure lactation, or on the mouth or throat, derived from contact with an infected infant, 34 have tubercles of the vulva, 19 syphilitic angina, 3 iritis, 14 tubercles of the vulva and angina simultaneously, 5 tubercles of the vulva, and others disseminated over other parts of the body, of divers complicated symptoms, 6 tubercles of the vulva, angina, tubercles on the skin, and iritis, and 19 no secondary symptoms.

In nurses, as well as in men infected with them, M. Rizzi has remarked that tubercles are the most common form of secondary symptoms, and angina is frequently superadded. A discharge, vegetations, and exostoses, are very rare, and buboes, when they occur, consist only of swelling and tension of the sub-maxillary or axillary glands.

In 53 infants, the disease manifested itself one month after birth in 33; at the expiration of two months in 11; of three months in 4; and in one only after the expiration of eight months. These statistics show how easily parties may be deceived as to the condition of infants that have been subject to the syphilitic poison, and how readily nurses may be exposed to the syphilitic poison from infants taken by them to nurse, without the slightest apprehension, whose parents even might not have a suspicion of the existence of the disease.—(Rankin's Abstract, Vol. v, p. 219, from Gaz. Med. di Milano, and Gaz. Med. de Paris, Oct. 24, 1846.)

On the 25th of October, 1858, a letter was addressed to the Imperial Academy of Medicine at Paris, by the Minister of Commerce, Agriculture, and Public Works, requesting an authoritative answer upon two questions: first, whether constitutional syphilis was contagious; and, secondly, whether, as regards contagion, there was a difference between constitutional syphilis as seen in infants at the breast and in adults. This letter led to the appointmant of a commission consisting of MM. Velpeau, Ricord, Devergie, Depaul, and Gilbert, and these commissioners reported and their report was adopted by the Academy,—first, that some of the manifestations of secondary syphilis, especially condylomata, are undoubtedly contagious; and, secondly, that there is no reason to suppose that the case is different in infants at the breast and in adults.

The commissioners arrived at this conclusion after examining the clinical facts and experimental researches already on record, and after four experiments of their own, which were undertaken with great reluctance on their part. The persons experimented upon were all suffering from lupus, but free from any syphilitic taint, and these were chosen from the notion that the treatment for syphilis, if the inoculation took effect, might possibly be of service in remedying the lupus.

The following case will serve as an example of the four experiments.

On a man, whose face had been affected with lupus from childhood, a raw surface was made on the left arm by strong ammonia, and to this was applied a piece of lint soaked in purulent matter obtained from a condyloma near the anus of a person who had had a chancre fifteen months previously. The condyloma was of fifteen days standing. Fourteen days afterwards there was slight redness at the seat of inoculation. Four days later still, a prominent coppery-colored papule made its appearance in the same part. On the twenty-second day this papule was much larger, and there was a slight oozing from the surface. During the week following the oozing, after being purulent, dried up into a thin scab. On the twenty-ninth day a gland in the corresponding axilla became enlarged. On the fifty-fifth day, the papule on the arm had become a real tubercle, with some slight ulceration in the centre, and several blotches and coppery papules had made their appearance on the trunk. During the week following, these papules became multiplied on the body, and they spread also to the extremities; many of them also changed into pustules of acne. Two or three days later the patient was put under the treatment for Syphilis, and in six weeks, at the date of the report, there was still much to be done in the way of a cure.

In addition to asserting the contagiousness of secondary Syphilis, the commission arrived at the conclusion, that there are characteristic grounds of distinction between the primary and secondary affection, and that the period of incubation in the secondary affection is from eighteen to twenty days, or even longer, and that the result is first a papule, and then a tubercle, which is finally converted into an ulcer covered with a crust.—(Rankin's Abstract, No. 30, p. 273, from Comptes Rendus, May 24th and 31st, 1849.

We might greatly multiply such facts from various authors, but this appears to be unnecessary, as the experience of the authors just quoted covers three centuries; and we are justified in affirming that it is now clearly established that constitutional Syphilis can be transmitted by direct inoculation with the secretions of secondary sores.

And recent experiments have shown that the blood of persons affected with constitutional Syphilis is capable when inoculated on healthy subjects of giving rise to syphilitic disease.

Waller succeeded in inoculating a healthy boy fifteen years old, with this disease, by applying the blood of an individual affected with secondary Syphilis to incisions made by a scarificator on the body of the boy. Well marked and unmistakable symptoms of secondary Syphilis followed this experiment. Other experimenters have arrived at similar results, but the best conducted experiments appear to be those performed by Professor Pelizzari,* of Italy.

As this subject is of great interest, we present the account of these experiments, as it is contained in one of the most recent works on Venerial Diseases :

This physician inoculated two medical students with the blood of a syphilitic patient with a negative result. On the 6th of February, 1862, he resumed his experiments, three physicians, Drs. Bargioni, Rosi, and Passagli submitting themselves to his investigations. The blood of a female patient, aged twenty-five, affected with constitutional syphilis, and who had undergone no treatment, was used for the purpose. The blood was drawn, with a new lancet, from the cephalic vein. The patient was at the time affected with mucous papules on the left labium, at the place where the chancre had existed; mucous tubercles surrounded the anus, and the inguinal glands were indurated and enlarged, and there were pustules on the head. At the point on the arm from which the blood was drawn there was no sign of any eruption, the skin of the part was well washed, and the surgeon washed his own hands. The bandage was new, as was also the vessel in which the blood was received. As the blood escaped from the cephalic vein, some of it was received on a piece of lint, which was placed on the upper part of Dr. Bargioni's arm, where the epidermis had previously been removed, and three transverse incisions made. A similar operation was performed on the other two gentlemen, but in the case of one the blood was cold, and in that of the other it had coagulated.

After twenty-four hours the dressings were removed, and nothing was observed but the crusts formed by the effused blood. Four days afterwards all traces of the inoculations had disappeared

On the morning of the third of March, Dr. Bargioni informed Prof. Pelizzari that in the center of the inoculated surface he had noticed a slight elevation, which produced a little itching. The arm was examined, and at the point indicated Prof. Pelizzari found a small papule of a roundish form, and of a dull-red color. On the eighth day the papule had augmented to the size of a twenty-centime piece. On the eleventh day it was covered with a very thin adherent scale, which became denser, and on the second day commenced to crack in its central part. On the fourteenth day two axillary glands became enlarged to the size of nuts. The papule remained indolent, and there was no induration at its base. On the twenty-first the scale was transferred into a true crust, and the part beneath was ulcerating. Slight induration was more evident. On the twenty-second the crust was detached, leaving a funnel-shaped ulcer, with elastic and resistant borders, forming an annular induration. There was but a small amount of secretion from the

---

* Lectures on Syphilis, by Henry Lee, 1863; p. 198.

sore, and the pain was trifling. On the twenty-sixth the ulcer had become as large as a fifty-centime piece, and the surrounding induration was considerably increased. Up to the 4th of April the ulcer remained stationary, but at that date its base appeared to be granulating. The axillary glands remained swollen, hard, and indolent. Slight nocturnal pains occurred in the head about this time, and the posterior cervical glands became somewhat enlarged. On the 12th of April spots of an irregular form and of rose color appeared on the surface of the body. The eruption extended itself, and during the succeeding days became more confluent. No constitutional disturbance, heat of skin, or pruritus accompanied it. On the twentieth the cervical glands had increased in size and were harder. The chancre maintained its specific character and exhibited no tendency to cicatrization. On the twenty second the color of the eruption was decidedly coppery. Small lenticular papules were now perceived to be mixed with the erythema. The edges of the chancre had begun to granulate. Mercury was now administered.

This case is of itself sufficient to prove the inoculability of syphilis through the blood of an infected person.

III. As we have before said, in the Third Section of this Inquiry, the acceptance without reserve of the doctrine of John Hunter, expressing the impossibility of the coëxistence of two actions, or two local diseases, or two different fevers, in the same part, or in the same constitution, at one and the same time, would necessarily lead to the denial of the possibility of transmitting Syphilis, through the medium of the matter produced by a distinct disease as cow-pox.

What are called pathological *laws*, are nothing more, than expressions of the fixed modes in which the phenomena of disease are manifested, and they conform to truth, only when they conform to, or formulate, the established course of nature. It is evident that a law may correctly express the relations of a certain class of facts and phenomena, without necessarily embracing other facts and phenomena, which upon a superficial view are related to those undoubtedly embraced by the law.

Whilst the law of Hunter may express the relations of the actions of the special poisons of the Exanthemata, (and we have shown in the third section, that it was from this very class of diseases, that the law was formulated,) it does not at all necessarily follow, that it is applicable to the actions of poisons differing wholly in their nature, mode of origin, and pathological actions.

The poison of Syphilis, after its introduction into the system, induces profound alterations in the blood, and in the processes of secretion and nutrition, and, in fact, produces derangement through all the solids and fluids. The economy under the action of constitutional Syphilis, is to be looked upon as entirely deranged. When, therefore, another disease is engrafted upon this state, the product of that diseased action, must partake, more or less, of the diseased condition of the blood and tissues. Does any one deny this, with reference to the products of inflammation excited in the syphilitic subject? Do not even our nosologies express this fact? Where is there sufficient proof to show, that syphilitic blood and lymph, furnishing materials for the elaboration of the vaccine matter, looses, altogether during this new process, its contagious and poisonous properties in the vaccine vesicle? Is not the vaccine vesicle but the manifestation of a general disease affecting the entire system, just as the eruptive skin affection of Syphilis, is the manifestation of a disease pervading the entire system? In addition to the facts recorded in this inquiry, is it not well known that the fetus in utero is affected by the vaccination of the mother? And it is probable, though experiments are as yet wanting, that the blood of one suffering with the vaccine disease, may propagate the disease by inoculation.

If then it be possible to produce a protective vaccine pustule, in an individual suffering from secondary Syphilis, then it is established that two local and two constitutional diseases may exist at the same time and in the same constitution, and the law of Hunter falls to the ground, as far as the action of these two animal poisons is concerned.

If the law of Hunter be universally applicable, we should have no vaccine disease produced at all, upon individuals suffering with constitutional Syphilis.

But even admitting that the special contagious matter of cowpox, formed from the blood of one suffering with constitutional Syphilis, is free from the poison of Syphilis, how can we practically, in the process of vaccination, separate this from all admixture with the diseased epithelial cells, cellular tissue, and syphilitic products of the skin and blood. If the dried scab be used, does not this cover, and in fact has it not been formed from a circumscribed portion of structure which had been originally tainted with Spyhilis, and are not its borders encrusted and mixed up with the products of the secondary diseased skin ?

The truth is, that we have much yet to learn about the phenomena manifested by the living organism when acted upon simultaneously by two or more poisons. Much of our established treatment, consists in the use of certain poisons to overcome the effects of other poisons, under which the system is laboring.

In this inquiry we do not need pathological formula, and generalizations, so much as well authenticated facts.

We cannot subscribe to the doctrine, that practically all danger may be avoided, by proper caution, as "every morbid appearance on the cutaneous envelope has its own peculiar character, by which it may be distinguished from other similar phenomena, and thus the observer may easily establish a distinction between the vaccine vesicle and other vesicular, bullar, or pustular eruptions." Is it not well known that Syphilis may lurk for years in one individual, never occasioning so much inconvenience as to arouse suspicion, until it is unmasked by the unexpected appearance of an infected offspring? On the other hand how fearfully rapid and destructive is the progress of the disease in others, in which from the first appearance of the chancre, symptom follows symptom, sore throat, swelled testicle, iritis, eruptions, nodes, ulcerations, and caries, until the entire body has become apparently a mass of filth and rottenness.

Both are examples of one disease, and examples of the action of the same poison; and we can only refer these differences to the peculiar states or conditions of different individuals.

We are utterly and profoundly ignorant of the variations on the vaccine vesicle under these different states of the constitution; and we are utterly and profoundly ignorant of those conditions which are essential to the transmission of the syphilitic poison through the medium of the vaccine vesicle.

But to the facts :—

About eleven years ago a medical man was condemned to two years imprisonment for having vaccinated several children from a child exhibiting a syphilitic eruption on its face and body. The witnesses asserted that the vaccine pustules had not been properly developed, and were followed by tedious ulcerations. Moreover, nine grown-up persons were asserted to have been re-infected by the children tainted through the vacine pustule.

The judgment was commuted in consequence of the opinions expressed by Messrs. Heyfelder and Pauli, two distinguished medical men of Rhenish Bavaria, whose judgment had been supported by that of Ricord and Cullerier, who utterly denied the possibility of communicating the syphilitic poison by the agency of vaccine lymph.—(B. & F. Med. Chirurg. Rev., Oct., 1855, from Bull. Gén. de Thérap., July, 1855.)

M. Viennois* has collected many cases of the transmission of Syphilis by vaccination, and has summed up his conclusions from the data on hand. From his observations and researches it would appear that Syphilis cannot be communicated by vaccine virus taken from a subject affected with the disease unless a portion of the blood of the individual is also inoculated. Thus he says:

"When the vaccine virus of a syphilitic subject, pure and unmixed with blood, is inoculated on a healthy individual, a simple vaccine pustule is obtained, without any near or remote syphilitic complications being produced.

"On the contrary, if, with the vaccine virus of a syphilitic individual who either has or has not at the time constitutional accidents, a healthy person is vaccinated, and the point of the lancet be charged with a little blood at the same time as with the vaccine virus, both diseases may be transmitted by the one operation—the vaccine disease with the vaccine virus, and Syphilis with the syphilitic disease."

M. Viennois also concludes that in such cases the vaccine vesicle is developed first, and that after undergoing its incubatory period the syphilitic ulcer, with all the characteristics of a true chancre, appears.

The following are the conclusions of M. Viennois.

1. Syphilis has in many instances been observed to follow vac-

---

* De la Transmission de la Syphilis par la Vaccination. Archiv. Gen. de Med., Juin, Juillet, et Septembre, 1860.

cination, ever since the introduction of that operation, and by authors worthy of credit, French, English, German, Italian, &c.

2. When a syphilitic subject is vaccinated, in whom the disease is in a latent state, syphilitic symptoms may be developed by the vaccine influence; these symptoms often consist in general eruptions of a papular, vesicular, or pustular character, but a chancre never forms at the seat of the vaccinal puncture.

3. On the contrary, if a healthy subject be vaccinated with vaccine virus taken from a syphilitic subject, and the lancet be charged at the same time with a little blood, as well as vaccine matter, the two diseases may be conveyed by the same puncture—the vaccine with the vaccine matter, and Syphilis with the syphilitic blood.

4. In these cases, of which a number are on record, vaccination is first developed because its period of incubation is shortest, and its evolution more rapid than that of Syphilis. The latter appears subsequently, and manifests itself by its characteristic lesion at the inoculated spot.

5. The initial lesion, then, by which Syphilis, following the vaccinal pustule, manifests itself, is an indurated ulcer, with adenitis; in a word, all the phenomena of primitive syphilitic chancre. The great law announced by M. Rollet, that Syphilis always commences by a chancre, even when it results from secondary symptoms, or even from syphilitic blood, is thus fully confirmed.

6. After the primary chancre is developed at the inoculated spot, and in the usual period, secondary Syphilis occurs, and runs the usual course, as if transmitted in any other way.

7. When the mixture of virus does not take place accidentally, but is affected intentionally, (as practiced by MM. Spéreno and Daumés, by mixing the vaccine matter with the pus of chancre,) the result is the same; one virus does not destroy the other, but each runs its separate course.

8. The vaccine matter thus acts as a simple vehicle for the virus contained in the syphilitic blood, which it divides and dilutes, as a drop of water would do, without at all modifying its properties or its effects.

9. It is important, then, never to take the vaccine virus from a suspected person, or from an infant whose parents are unknown before the age at which hereditary Syphilis usually manifests itself.

10. If circumstances make this last necessary, great care should be taken to collect only the vaccine matter, free from blood or any syphilitic humour.

11. In no case should a healthy subject be vaccinated with matter taken from a syphilitic subject, for in spite of all precautions, there can be no certainty as to the purity of the vaccine matter.

12. These precautions are the more important, because, with the matter from one syphilitic subject a number of persons may be vaccinated, and Syphilis conveyed to nearly all, (as seen by Ceriale, of Cremona.)

13. It is sufficient to point out these precautions, to avoid new evils, and to remove the cavils of the enemies of vaccination; for in these cases, the propagation of Syphilis is not the fault of vaccination, but of the vaccinator.—(Gaz. Méd. de Paris, Jan. 26, 1861. American Journal of Medical Sciences, April, 1861.)

These views of M. Viennois have recently received the most ample confirmation from the tragedy which occurred at Rivalta, in Italy, by which forty-six children and twenty nurses had syphilis communicated to them through vaccination, and of which several of the children died. The full details of this remarkable event are given in a memoir by Dr. Pacchiotti,* of Turin, and the following summary from his report is given from Dr. Hammond's recent work.

On the 21st of May, 1861, Sig. Caglola vaccinated Giovanni Chiabrera with lymph contained in a tube sent from Aequi. The operation was performed in the usual manner and with a perfectly clean lancet. The child was eleven months old, and in good health at the time. Forty-six other children were, ten days subsequently, vaccinated with the lymph taken from the vesicle of this child; and ten days after this, seventeen children were vaccinated with lymph taken from the arm of Luigia Manzone, one of the forty-six first vaccinated.

Of these sixty-three children, forty-six—thirty-nine of the first lot and seven of the last—were within two months attacked with Syphilis. On the 7th of October seven of them, including the little Manzone, were dead, three were yet in danger of dying, fourteen were recovering under the use of mercury and iodine, and one was well.

* Sifilide trasmissa per Mezzo della Vaccinazione in Rivalta, presso Aequi. Gazetta della Associazone Med., Octobre 20, 1861.

A medical commission was now appointed to inquire into all the circumstances connected with this fatal event, and they proceeded to the execution of the duty assigned them.

Twenty-three children were examined in full; the others were not so accurately noticed, as their parents had neglected to avail themselves of medical aid in time. In the forty-six children who were affected, Syphilis appeared at periods varying from ten days to two months after vaccination, the average time being twelve days. The initiatory symptoms were variable. Sometimes just as the vaccine vesicle had healed, it became surrounded with a red, livid, and copper-colored areola, and ulcerated again. In other instances an ulcer would form on the cicatrix, and become covered with a scab, which in a few days would fall off to make room for another, and so on. In others the vaccine vesicles had an unhealthy appearance from the first, and were accompanied by a general eruption.

The principal symptoms observed by the commission were mucous tubercles in the vicinity of the anus and on the genitals, ulcerations of the mucous membrane of the lips and fauces, engorgement of the lymphatic glands in the groin and neck, syphilitic skin diseases, alopecia, deep tubercles, gummy tumors, etc.

In two subsequent papers, Dr. Pachiotti* continues the detail of his investigations. On the 8th of February, twenty of the mothers or nurses of the forty-six children had become affected with symptoms of Syphilis. He ascertained, too, from a revaccination of five of the children, that the occurrence of Syphilis had not destroyed the efficacy of the first vaccination. But he also discovered the source of the infection. It appeared that a year and a half previously a young unmarried woman had had Syphilis, and that she was syphilitic at the time Chiabrera was vaccinated. This woman was the mother of a child which had died syphilitic three months after its birth. After the death of the child she was in the habit of having her breasts drawn by the little Chiabrera, and gave him the clothes which her own child had worn. Another child nursed by this woman, but who was not vaccinated, also became syphilitic, and this child infected its mother just as little Chiabrera did his mother. It is therefore shown that the vaccine virus used on Chiabrera was not at fault, but that all the other forty-five children were infected through the lymph taken from his arm. It is also shown that blood was on the lancet when several of the children were vaccinated.

Dr. Pacchiotti, as the results of his investigations and those of the commission, gives the following rules to be observed in vaccinating:—

1st. Examine the child from whom the lymph is taken.

2d. Inquire into the state of the parent's health.

3d. Take the lymph in preference from those children who have passed the fourth or fifth month, as hereditary Syphilis appears in general before that time.

4th. Do not use lymph taken from a vesicle which has passed its eighth day, because on the ninth and tenth days the lymph becomes mixed with pus, which latter may be of an infectious character.

5th. In taking the lymph, avoid hemorrhage, as there is less danger with lymph free from blood.

6th. Do not vaccinate too many children with the same lymph.

In consequence of the publication of the details of the lamentable affair at Rivalta, Dr. Marone concluded to relate the particulars of a similar event which occurred to him, and in regard to which he had thought it advisable to maintain a discreet silence. The particulars are given with sufficient fullness by Mr. Lee, whose excellent work I have already referred to several times.

It seems that in November, 1856, Dr. Marone obtained some vaccine lymph, with which he vaccinated a number of children at Lupara. The lymph was contained in glass tubes, and Dr. Marone noticed that it was mixed with a little blood, which affected its transparency. Of the number of children vaccinated with this lymph, notes were preserved in twenty-three cases. All these were affected with Syphilis, and the disease likewise manifested itself among the mothers, nurses, and even the servants who were brought in contact with them. The symptoms with which the children were affected consisted chiefly of eruptions of a syphilitic character, and sub

---

*L'Union Medicale, Fev. 5eme et Avril 3eme, 1862.

sequently of mucous tubercles at the angles of lips, around the anus, and on the vulva. The post-cervical and inguinal glands were enlarged, and there was emaciation, in degree varying with the severity of the syphilitic symptoms.

Besides these cases, eleven nurses of the number who suckled these children gave the disease to eleven other children who were not vaccinated.

In some of the cases the syphilitic phenomena continued till April, 1859.

Dr. Marone draws the following conclusions from his experience:—

"That the syphilitic virus was really transmitted in the above recorded cases by means of vaccination.

"That the children vaccinated suffered first, and became the means of transmitting the disease to others.

"That the lymph used for the purpose of vaccination was impure, being mixed with blood, and that the result shows how necessary it is to abstain from using lymph of that description.'

—*Lectures on Venereal Diseases: By Wm. A. Hammond, M. D. Philadelphia: J. B. Lippincott & Co.*, 1864. *pp.* 208, 217.

And whilst these pages are passing through the press, we read in the Medical News and Library that Syphilis has recently been extensively propagated by vaccination in France.

In a western department of France, (Morbihan,) some villages have been the theatre of severe syphilitic symptoms in more than thirty children, who had all been vaccinated from a little girl with six punctures on each arm, the child herself having been operated upon from another who had been vaccinated from lymph preserved between two plates of glass obtained from the authorities. This misfortune created so much sensation, that the Academy of Medicine of Paris, sent down two commissioners, Messrs. Henry Rogu and Depaul. These gentlemen have just presented their report to the Academy, and this important document ends with the following considerations:

1. Several of the children whom we have examined were undoubtedly suffering from secondary Syphilis.

2. We see no way of explaining this contamination but by vaccination, and we are confident that the cases we have seen were really Syphilis engendered by vaccination.

3. As to the origin of the virus, it is very probable that the poison is traceable to the lymph, preserved between two pieces of glass, supplied by the authorities.

As primary symptoms were also observed among the children M. Ricord begged the commissioners to insert that fact in thei report, which these gentlemen agreed to do. Here we unfortunately have again repeated the sad occurrences which took place at Rivalta, (Italy,) a short time ago.—(Medical News and Library, 1867—from London Lancet, Dec. 15, 1866.)

The experience of the Confederate Surgeons, establishing the possibility of communicating constitutional Syphilis by vaccination; the experiments of Waller, Pelizzari and others, establishing the possibility of communicating secondary Syphilis by inoculation of the blood from patients suffering with the constitutional symptoms of this disease into healthy individuals: the cases collected by M. Viennois illustrating the transmission of Syphilis by vaccination: and the unfortunate tragedy of Rivalta in the district of Piedmont, Italy, where Syphilis was previously unknown, (forty-six children of various ages being simultaneously attacked with well-marked Syphilis, proceeding in all cases which could be properly examined from the action of vaccine virus which produced chancre on the arms, followed by buboes in the axilla, and all these children had been vaccinated directly or indirectly from a single child, who was subsequently proved to have contracted Syphilis from a wet nurse, and these children transmitted the disease to a number of women, their wet nurses and mothers, and even to children who played and nursed with them, and the women so infected, in turn infected their husbands, and finally the disease yielded in all cases to the usual remedies for Syphilis:) these, and other similar facts, as the infection of the infant at the breast with secondary Syphilis, and the communication of Syphilis from the infant inheriting the disease from its mother or father, to a healthy nurse,—all demonstrate the possibility of transmitting constitutional Syphilis by inoculation of syphilitic blood, or vaccine virus, from patients poisoned with Syphilis; and each such fact, of itself is sufficient to overthrow the dogma, that "Primary Syphilis alone is capable of being inoculated, and that secondary affections and the constitutional disease cannot be communicated from one individual to another, by any such means as vaccination, or the direct inoculation of syphilitic blood."

CONTENTS.

SECTION I.—Preliminary Observations—Accidents attending Vaccination amongst the Citizens and Soldiers of the Confederate States—Necessity for the Investigation—Method, extent and object of the Inquiry, - - - - - - - 3–11
The injurious effects of Vaccination referred to six causes, 4–5
Circular Letter addressed to the Medical Officers of the late Confederate Army, - - - - - - - 5–6
Facts illustrating the value of Vaccination, and the fatality of Small-Pox, - - - - - - - - 7–8
Description of Small-Pox, by Sir Matthew Hale, - - 8
Dr. Jenner pointed out some causes of the accidents attending Vaccination and gave rules for their avoidance, - - 9–11

SECTION II.—Modification, Alteration and Degeneration of the Vaccine Vesicle, dependent upon depressed and deranged forces, resulting from fatigue, exposure and poor diet; and upon an impoverished, vitiated and scorbutic condition of the Blood of the patients vaccinated and yielding vaccine matter, - 12–33
In Scorbutic Patients all Injuries of the Skin tend to form ulcers of an unhealthy character; effects of Scurvy upon the character and progress of the Vaccine Vesicle, - - 12–13
Investigations upon the effects of Vaccination amongst the Federal Prisoners confined in Camp Sumpter, Andersonville, Ga., - - - - - - - - 13–27
Examination of the charge urged by the United States Military Commission, that the Confederate Surgeons deliberately poisoned or destroyed the Federal prisoners at Andersonville with poisonous Vaccine Matter, - - - 13–27
Dr. Hamilton on Spurious Vaccination in the U. S. Army, - 26
Dr. L. Guild on the Medical Records of the Army of Northern Virginia, - - - - - - - - 27
Report on Spurious Vaccination in the Confederate Army, by S. E. Habersham, M.D., of Augusta, Ga., - - - 28

SECTION III.—The Employment of Matter from Pustules or Ulcers which had deviated from the regular and normal course of development of the Vaccine Vessicle; such deviation or imperfection in the Vaccine Disease and Pustule, being due mainly to previous Vaccination, and the existence of some Eruptive Disease at the time of Vaccination. Or, in other words, the employment of Matter from patients who had been previously Vaccinated, and were partially protected, or who were affected with some skin disease at the time of the insertion of the Vaccine Virus, - - - 84–59
Prof. Paul F. Eve, M.D., on Spurious Vaccination. - . 35
Dr. R. D. Hamilton, of Chattanooga, on Spurious Vaccination amongst the Confederate forces serving in East Tennessee, 36–38
Investigations of Dr. Edward Jenner, on the Varieties and Modifications of the Vaccine Disease, - - - 38–41
Answer to Dr. Jenner's Inquiries, by the Rector of Leckhamstead, - - - - - - - - 39–40
Observations of Dr. James Davis, of Columbia, South Carolina, on the Vaccine and Varioloid Disease, - - - 41–44

134

  Examination of the Doctrine of John Hunter, on Diseased
   Actions as being incompatible with each other, - - 45–59
  Relations of the Vaccine Disease to Measles and other dis-
   eases, with the observations of numerous authors, - - 47–57

SECTION IV.—Dried Vaccine Lymph, or Scabs, in which Decomposition has
  been excited by carrying the Matter about the person for a
  length of time, and thus subjecting it to a warm moist atmosphere, - - - - - - - - 59–62

SECTION V.—The mingling of the Vaccine Virus with that of the Small-pox;
  Matter taken from those who were vaccinated while they
  were laboring under the action of the poison of Small-pox
  was capable of producing a modified variola, and comparatively mild disease in the inoculated, and was capable of
  communicating by effluvia Small-pox in its worst character
  to the unprotected, - - - - - - 63-72
  Observations of Drs. Jenner, Woodville, Adams, Willan, Gregorie, Hennen, Fowler, and Bousquet, upon the relations of
  the Vaccine Disease and Small-pox, - - - 64–72

SECTION VI.—Dried Vaccine Lymph and Scabs, from Patients who had suf-
  fered with Erysipelas during the progress of the Vaccine
  Disease, or whose systems were in a depressed state from
  improper diet, bad ventilation, and the exhalations from
  Typhoid Fever, Erysipelas, Hospital Gangrene, Pyæmia, and
  offensive suppurating Wounds, - - - - 72–86
  Dr. Wm. Gerdner, of Greene County, Tenn., on the relations
  of Erysipelas to Vaccination, - - - - - 73
  Cases of Erysipelas following Vaccination, - - - - 74–78
  Views of Dr. Paul F. Eve, on the possibility of Inoculating
  Erysipelas by Vaccination, - - - - - 78
  Dr. J. C. Nott, of Mobile, Ala., on Erysipelas, - - - 80
  Report of Dr. J. F. Bell, of Virginia, - - - - 81
  Report of Surgeon Hunter McGuire of Virginia, - - 83

SECTION VII.—Fresh and Dried Vaccine Lymph and Scabs from Patients
  suffering with Secondary or Constitutional Syphilis at the
  time and during the process of Vaccination and the Vac-
  cine Disease, - - - - - - - 86–121
  Prof. S. M. Bemiss, M.D., of New Orleans, on the relations of
  Syphilis to Spurious Vaccination, - - - - 89
  Prof. Eve, Drs. Kratz, Fuqua, Ramsey, Crawford, Percival,
  Stout, Woodward and Hubbard, on the relations of Syphi-
  lis to Spurious Vaccination, - - - - - 90–105
  Discussion of the relations of Secondary or Constitutional
  Syphilis to Vaccination, - - - - - 105–132
  The possibility of communicating Tuberculosis and Cancer
  by Inoculation, - - - - - - - 107–109
  The possibility of communicating Secondary or Constitutional
  Syphilis by Inoculation, - - - - - - 110–124
  Testimony of Torella, 1498, William Clowes, 1637, Gideon
  Harvey, 1665, Daniel Turner, 1717, John Hunter, 1776, and
  of Drs. Duncan, Watson, Hamerton, Egan, Price, Rizzi, Wal-
  ler and others, on the contagiousness of Secondary Syphi-
  lis, - - - - - - - - - 110–124
  The possibility of communicating Constitutional Syphilis
  through the medium of the Vaccine Virus, - - 124–221
  Testimony of M. Viennois, Drs. Pacchiotti, Marone, Pogue
  and Depaul, - - - - - - - 127–131

www.ingramcontent.com/pod-product-compliance
Lightning Source LLC
Chambersburg PA
CBHW020105170426
43199CB00009B/397